To my dear
Birthday li
many happy ours of reading
with love from your everloving
firstborn Dorothy Ann, Keith, family

History of the
WELSH MILITIA AND
VOLUNTEER CORPS
1757 - 1908

Volume 3

By the same author

Glamorgan - Its Gentlemen and Yeomanry, 1797-1980

Welsh Militia and Volunteer Corps, 1757-1908
Volume 1: Anglesey and Caernarfonshire
Volume 2: The Glamorgan Regiments of Militia

Owen Roscomyl and the Welsh Horse

History of the
Welsh Militia and Volunteer Corps
1757 - 1908

Volume 3
Glamorgan (Part 2)

VOLUNTEERS & LOCAL MILITIA, 1796-1816
YEOMANRY CAVALRY, 1808-1831

by

Bryn Owen

bridge
books

Wrexham, Clwyd

First published in Wales by
BRIDGE BOOKS
61 Park Avenue
Wrexham, Clwyd
LL12 7AW

ISBN 1 872424 34 1

A CIP catalogue entry for this book
is available from the British Library

Printed and bound by
Longdunn Press Ltd
Bristol

CONTENTS

ILLUSTRATIONS

PREFACE

This volume is the third of a series which will place on record an account of the services of the militia regiments and volunteer corps of Wales during the 18th and 19th centuries and the first decade of the present century – a record which, in spite of its close connection with the changing social history of the principality, has to date been very much neglected. This record is intended to appeal not only to those who will be interested in the military activities of their forefathers, but also to local and family historians as an aid to further research.

To be prepared for war in time of peace is to my mind an eminently sensible precaution and one that sadly will be necessary for as long as certain men or political factions seek to impose their will upon others by means of the bomb and bullet. History has shown that such preparations, often in the face of considerable opposition, have ensured for the inhabitants of Great Britain a continuation of the freedoms which we all demand and cherish. The Welsh contribution to that end has throughout been considerable and has given to the principality a military heritage which is second to none.

This volume is dedicated to the men and women of Wales who gave unstinting and valuable service to their country during the two great wars of the present century and, in particular, to those whose roots were in the county of Glamorgan.

Bryn Owen
Radyr
Cardiff
1994

ACKNOWLEDGEMENTS

A Brookman; W Y Carman, FSA, FRHistS; Major J L Balmer, TD; Mike Chappell; P J Haythornthwaite; Major A G Harfield, BEM, FRHistS; Dr J Carey Hughes; H L King; C Lewis; N Litchfield; P MacLachlan, DL; D Pickup; J Tyler; R Westlake; Cardiff Central Library; Cyfarthfa Castle Museum, Merthyr Tydfil; Flatholm Trust; Glamorganshire County Records Office; Gloucester Central Library; Gwent County Records Office; Hereford Central Library; Ministry of Defence Central Library; National Museum of Wales, St Fagan's Castle; Royal Institute of South Wales, Swansea; Wallis & Wallis, Lewes, Sussex; Welch Regiment Museum, Cardiff Castle and the many others who, over several decades, have provided leads and snippets of information to assist my research.

Chapter 1
GLAMORGAN PROVISIONAL CAVALRY
1796 - c1799

Very little is recorded concerning this cavalry force, a form of horse militia established by Act 37, Geo lll, 1796. Intended as an additional reserve force for the defence of the kingdom, the idea was unpopular from the start, drawing little support, particularly from the landowning class and those who kept horses for business or other purposes. The Act required that every person owning ten horses on which duty was paid, should provide for the Provisional Cavalry of a county, one trooper, fully clothed, accoutred and suitably mounted and that those persons owning less than ten horses join with persons similarly situated in providing likewise.

The Act was even less popular with those who were expected to serve as Provisional Cavalrymen, as they were to be selected by ballot. On selection they were obliged to take the oath of allegiance and produce themselves for training at times and places selected by the Lord Lieutenant. When drawn out in the King's service they would receive pay at the rate paid to the regular cavalry, and were liable to certain penalties if they failed to appear for training, or did so improperly equipped and accoutred. So unpopular was the Act that within the course of the same year, it was amended to produce a compromise of sorts. By the amending Act, the Lords Lieutenant of counties who could produce as volunteers three quarters of the number of Provisional Cavalrymen required from their counties, were empowered to dispense with the Provisional Cavalry ballot and to substitute instead troops of Volunteer or Yeomanry Cavalry.

That the Act was for a time enforced in Glamorgan is supported by the Penrice and Margam MSS [1] which include details of a commission granted to one Hopkin Llewelyn of Pyle to be a Lieutenant in the Provisional Cavalry, and secondly the diary of John Perkins, farmer of Llantrithyd [2] who on 9 December 1796, wrote, "Settled Articles for providing a Man and a Horse for the Cavalry". On the 14th, he records his attendance at a meeting in St Nicholas, convened for the purpose of selecting a man to serve. He later wrote "The Lot fell on Evan William of St George's", which man, together with Lt Llewelyn, likely have the distinction of being the only two persons known by name to have served in Glamorgan's Provisional Cavalry. It is doubtful if either of the two were greatly inconvenienced as, by 1799, there were sufficient Yeomanry Cavalry active in the county to allow the Lord Lieutenant to take advantage of the Amending Act and thereby shelve the Provisional Cavalry ballot.

Provisional Cavalry corps, like Fencible Cavalry had six troops per regiment, but of those raised only six [3], of which none were Welsh, were embodied for garrison duty. In Glamorgan, any assembly would have been of short duration and confined solely to the needs of training. In respect of dress and equipment Provisional Cavalrymen were dressed and accoutred in very much the same style as Yeomanry Cavalry. No description of the colour and facings of their uniform dress has been found.

This unpopular and short-lived force was described by the historian Fortescue in the following terms:

> The Provisional Cavalry passed over the country like a blight. It was a pleasant conceit to make every man mount another's horse, till at length, when Men and Horses were brought together, no man knew how to mount, and so they all separated. [4]

Notes

1. Penrice & Margam, MSS 83/6.Vol II, p320, 9157 Red Box 29, NLW.
2. Perkins Diary, Welsh Folk Museum, Farming and Rural Life Collection.
3. Berkshire, Kent, Somerset, Suffolk, Northumberland & Worcestershire. Note 1036, *Journal of the Society for Army Historical Research*, Vol XXX, No 123, Autumn 1952.
4. Fortescue, J W, *History of the British Army*, Vol IV, part 2, p891.

Chapter 2
THE SEA FENCIBLES, 1798 - 1813

Bradstow [1] in his article *The Sea Fencibles* states that the innovator of this coast defence force was Captain Home Riggs Popham, RN, who in 1793 had commanded a small force of longshoremen and naval volunteers during the Flanders campaign. Pitt the Younger, a great supporter of the volunteer movement, was also active in encouraging the raising of Coastal Fencibles in the Cinque Ports of which he at one time was Warden [2].

On 14 March 1798, the King gave approval for the formation of a Corps of Sea Fencibles, as a result of which it did not take long for such units to make their appearance on the coast, including that of South Wales. Such units were to be found at points ranging from Chepstow to Fishguard but sadly, the records of their numbers and daily activities are almost non-existent. However, it is known that Swansea was very active in that field, with Commander John Jones, RN, being appointed to command the Sea Fencibles in that town on 24th December 1798.

Derived from the Latin *Defensible Personis*, the term 'Fencible' in 1483 described a male person between the age of 16 and 60 capable of bearing arms and recruited for local defence, which description fits well the Sea Fencible. By 1798 however, the term 'Fencible' described a different category of man, namely troops serving on terms very similar to regular soldiers for the duration of hostilities [3] and mainly committed only to serve within the bounds of the United Kingdom. It was a term often used incorrectly in the titles of various volunteer corps, and consequently, perhaps the title Royal Naval Coast Volunteers which was used to describe a later corps, would have been a more accurate description.

Enrolled from seafaring men resident along the coast, the Sea Fencibles were by all accounts the most versatile and aggressive of the volunteer corps of the period. A tough, hard living bunch, most were no strangers to fighting and violence, due to the conditions of their calling and involvement in the smuggling trade. Administered by the Board of Admiralty, the senior officers were ex-Royal Navy men on half pay - men not required for active service with the fleet due to age or partial disability from past wounds. Other officers were, like Volunteer officers, appointed locally, from men of property and standing.

Apart from certain Pembrokeshire volunteer units, who in February 1797 confronted the French near Fishguard, the Sea Fencibles appear to be the only other arm of the Volunteer force to come to grips with the enemy. No incidents of that nature were recorded on the South Wales coast, but on the south east coast of England, Sea Fencibles are known to have been in action against French privateers [4].

Like other volunteer corps (Yeomanry excepted), the Sea Fencibles appear to have stood down following the signing of the Peace of Amiens in 1802. Only one or two press reports have been found which make brief mention of the Glamorgan corps up to that date.

The *Hereford Journal* in 1803 confirms that Sea Fencibles had been re-mustered, and were once again active in Glamorgan following the resumption of hostilities against France in March of that year.

> The Sea Fencibles are intended to comprise all Fishermen and other persons occupied in the Ports and on the Coasts, who from their calling are not likely to be impressed. Forty eight Port Captains and Commanders, with an appropriate number of Lieutenants were appointed to this service around the island; and in South Wales, from Chepstow in Monmouthshire to the mouth of the Bristol Channel, rendezvous at Swansea under the command of Captain Richard Jones and Captain George Jones. [5]

In October the same news-sheet stated:

The Sea Fencible Corps of that County (Glamorgan) are improving rapidly in numbers and discipline. [6]

At the turn of the present century, a Miss P E Simons having interviewed many elderly residents of the Gower concerning their recollections of times gone by, wrote up the result of her findings for a Gower parish magazine:

> The Mr Talbot of the time (I presume Ivor Talbot) raised a body of Sea Fencibles to protect the coast against a possible invasion by Napoleon, and when the invasion scare was at its height, the Portheynon men were encamped on a portion of the Burrows lying under Point Mine (in front of the Undrils), which is now known as the Boiling Green. In front of the Camp was a ditch of defence. When I knew it first, it was perhaps 6' deep and 6' wide at the top. Here they had a gay time, the Womenfolk going to visit their men taking food and drink, and they used to dance the night through. When a man joined these Sea Fencibles, the rest of the Corps met in solemn conclave and decided a nickname for the new member. Two men were then deputised to see the newcomer and 'bring him to his name'.
>
> There was no Mr then, just plain Sam or John. Thenceforward he was known by it and practically dropped his own name. These Sea Fencibles were armed with Swords. I have seen two of them, but I think that they have already disappeared by now.

The parishioners recollections referred to the Portheynon detachment of the Swansea Sea Fencible Corps in the period 1803-04.

The Admiralty provided the Sea Fencibles with galleys - large open boats propelled by 40 oarsmen, which had an 18lb-cannon mounted in the bows. The galleys were moored in convenient harbours or inlets and were kept ready for instant action.

In July 1804, the *Cambrian*, with reference to Swansea, stated:

> Two Brass Field Pieces with their Carriages etc, complete, arrived here on Saturday last (7 July, 1804) to be attached to the Sea Fencibles of this Port. [7]

Provision of cannon with field carriages illustrates the versatility of these coast defence corps. Armed with cutlasses, pistols, muskets and boarding pikes, they, like Marines, were equally at home on both sea or land. The two cannon on reconstructed carriages, have survived the passage of time and today look out over the terrace of the Mansion House in Swansea.

Like other volunteer units of the period, the Sea Fencibles were subject to periodic inspection, one such event taking place in October 1804 when Admiral Phillips inspected the Swansea and Portheynon contingents as well as vessels of the Naval Imprest Service operating out of the port. [8]

That Sea Fencibles were a force to be reckoned with was confirmed by the *Cambrian* which reassured its invasion concious readers:

> In the case of emergency, no description of force in this Kingdom is likely to render more effectual service in this country than this useful body of men. From habit

and avocation they are inured to the weather in its utmost inclemency, and judging by the zeal of those in this quarter [Swansea], everything may fairly be expected from their courage and alacrity. [9]

The victory at Trafalgar in October 1805, not only removed for the duration the threat of invasion, but also cut off at one stroke the very reason for Sea Fencible existence. They continued in service nevertheless and in August 1807, Captain F F Gardner, RN, succeeeded Captain Richard Jones, RN, as Commandant of the Sea Fencibles in the Chepstow/Swansea district. [10]

Confirmation that the Portheynon detachment were still active in 1808 is given in the *Cambrian* which, in March of that year, reported that Lieutenant Williams and members of the Portheynon Corps had subscribed a day's pay for the relief of one David Morgan who had been injured in a local quarry. [11] At this point the press becomes silent and nothing more is reported on Sea Fencible activities. Between 1809 and 1812, the force was slowly run down and had likely disappeared entirely in South Wales by 1813. Their like was not to be seen again for almost forty years and the formation of a somewhat similar body styled Royal Naval Coast Volunteers.

Although having no unbroken lineal connection with the later Royal Naval Coast Volunteers, Royal Naval Artillery Volunteers, Royal Naval Reserve Volunteers and so through to the Royal Naval Volunteer Reserve, those South Wales Sea Fencibles of the late 18th and early 19th centuries can, in my opinion, be justifiably called the forerunners of the present South Wales Division, Royal Naval Reserve.

In respect of dress, the Sea Fencibles looked very much like the Royal Navy sailors of their day. Officers dress was similar in all respects to that of a serving naval officer. The men wore a tarred sennet hat bearing the painted badge of the corps. They were also supplied with a short double breasted jacket, a wool jumper with blue and white horizontal stripes, a pair of white duck trousers and a strong pair of buckled leather shoes. Around

Shoulder belt plate, Corps of Sea Fencibles, c1804.

17

A Glamorgan Ranger, c1800 (left) and a Swansea Sea Fencible, c1804 (right) by M Chappell.

the waist they wore a broad leather belt with brass buckle from which was suspended the cutlass frog and scabbard.

Notes

1. Bradstow, 'The Sea Fencibles', in *Guns,Weapons and Militaria*,Vol I, No II, October 1982.
2. Cousins G, *The Defenders*, F Muller, London 1968.
3. Fortescue, J W, *History of the British Army*,Vol IV, Pt 1, p83.
4. Bradstow, ibid.
5. *Hereford Journal*, 13 July 1803.
6. Ibid, 19 October 1803.
7. *Cambrian*, 13 July 1804.
8. Ibid, 12 October 1804.
9. Ibid, 4 May 1804.
10. Ibid, 24 August 1807.
11. Ibid, 11 March 1808.

Chapter 3
THE VOLUNTEER MOVEMENT, 1794 - 1802

Few records relating to the organisation and activities of the volunteers of 1794-1802 or of the second phase, 1803-08, are preserved locally. To search in any depth, one must visit the Public Records Office, Kew where, among the mass of War Office and Home Office correspondence a great deal of information can be found including a list of the various corps and the names of those appointed as officers and the dates of their commissions. In some counties, the Letter Books kept by the Clerks to the Lieutenancy have survived, several of which contain Volunteer records. It is said that Letter Books compiled by a Clerk of the Lieutenancy of Glamorgan survive in private hands, but sadly it has not been my privilege to study and quote from them. Before going on to list and discuss the various corps it will be necessary to give the reader some idea of the circumstances in which they were raised, and of the laws and regulations which governed their activities.

The year 1794, found Great Britain at war with Revolutionary France, and with the government of the day much concerned about the extensive military preparations then taking place on the French Channel coast – activities quite obviously directed towards an invasion of Britain. The situation was in many ways similar to that which Britain faced half a century ago when she stood alone, facing across the same narrow strip of sea, the armed might of Hitler's Germany. At the close of the 18th century there was also uncertainty at home, with fears that

MONMOUTHSHIRE.

CONDITIONS

ON WHICH

ASSOCIATED CORPS

ARE TO BE RAISED FOR THE

Defence of the Country.

Associated Corps to be raised in Cities and Towns,

Are to confit of none but known refpectable Houfeholders, or Perfons who can bring at leaft two fuch Houfeholders to anfwer for their good Behaviour.

Such Armed Affociations either of Cavalry or Infantry, if recommended by the Lord Lieutenant, will be accepted by his Majefty, *although the Offer of their Services should be be limited respectively to the Town in which they are to be raised, and within a few miles thereof.*

The Officers of the faid Corps, will receive Commiffions from the King, upon the Recommendation of the Lord Lieutenant; and if required, Arms will be fupplied by Government, but every other Expence of Armed Affociations of this Defcription muft be defrayed by themfelves.

Country Associations.

No Volunteer to be admitted into the Armed Affociations to be formed in the Country, whofe habitual Occupation and Place of Refidence is not within the Divifion of the County to which the Affociation may extend.

Horse Associations.

That thofe who may prefer Service on Horfeback, fhall (if the Troops of Yeomanry already raifed within the County fhould not be compleated, or fhould their prefent Eftablifhment admit, without Inconvenience, of an Augmentation) be received into the neareft Troop of the fame, in all Cafes where this Arrangement may fuit local Purpofes, and be found acceptable to the faid Troops, and to the Parties: and in other Cafes they will be formed into feparate and independent Troops of not lefs than 40, or more than 80 Men each, to be commanded by fuch Officers as may be recommended by the Lord Lieutenant, in a fimilar Proportion to the Yeomanry Cavalry, and they will be entitled to the fame Allowances and Affiftance from Government, to procure Clothing and Appointments, at the Rate of Three Pounds for each Man ferving in the faid Corps, per Annum, for three Years, fubject to the fame Regulations, and to be iffued in the fame Manner as to the Yeomanry Cavalry already clothed. All new Troops formed upon this Principle, to engage to be trained at leaft once a Week, and for not lefs than THREE Hours at a Time, and in Cafe of actual Invafion, or the actual Appearance of an Enemy upon the Coaft, to ferve within the Limits of the Military Diftrict to which they belong.

Foot Associations.

The Armed Affociations of Infantry are propofed to be formed into Independent Companies of not lefs than 60, nor more than 120 Men in each Company, to be armed in the fame Manner as the Volunteer Corps in the Towns; or fhould it be found impoffible from their Number to furnifh them all with Mufquets in the firft Inftance, that a certain Proportion fhall be provided with Pikes; that they fhall be provided with an Uniform Clothing, or a fair Allowance to provide themfelves with it, at the Public Expence; Each Company to be commanded by a Captain, to be recommended by the Lord Lieutenant, having a Lieutenant, an Enfign, and a proper Number of Non-commiffioned Officers, in Proportion to the Strength of the Company under him; The Lord Lieutenant is not to recommend any Perfon to fuch Command, but thofe who have a Refidence and an Income in Land to the Amount of FIFTY POUNDS a Year, within the County, or thofe who rent Land within the fame to the Amount of ONE HUNDRED POUNDS per Annum, and, if poffible, within the Divifion thereof, in which fuch Company may be raifed, or the Sons of Perfons fo qualified, or Perfons having previoufly held fome Military Commiffion, which in the Lord Lieutenant's Judgment might render them eligible for fuch Situation, although they may not hold Land either in Poffeffion or Occupancy to the Amount above-mentioned. The Lord Lieutenant may recommend, for Subaltern Officer's Commiffions, Perfons accuftomed to Military Service, and they will be preferred; and in Cafe no proper Perfon of this Defcription fhould be known to his Lordfhip, Government will endeavour, as far as poffible, to provide one, together with One Non-commiffioned Officer for each Company, to train the Men, and teach them the Ufe of Arms. This Non-commiffioned Officer, to receive conftant Pay from Government. The Subaltern Officer, if folected from the Half-Pay Lift, to be allowed the full Pay of his Rank, and in Cafe he has heretofore been engaged in any Military Line not entitling him to Half-Pay, he will, if approved of, be entitled to an Allowance equivalent to the Half-Pay of whatever Commiffion he may hold in the Company, fo long as he fhall continue to hold fuch Commiffion: Each Company of Infantry, to engage to be trained at leaft once a Week, and for not lefs than THREE Hours at a Time, and in Cafe of Invafion, to ferve within the Limits of the SEVERN Military Diftrict, in which this County is included. Every Man will be entitled (fhould he think proper to claim it) to an Allowance of One Shilling per Week, to be paid by Government, to fuch as may appear upon the Return figned by the Commanding Officer, as having attended at the Mufter and Training above-mentioned.

Printed notice relating to Armed Associations, c1798. [Gwent County Record Office]

Jacobin sympathisers would exploit working class disaffection to incite internal disorder. With the greater part of the regular army on, or committed to foreign service, the main force available to the government to face invasion and internal emergency, was an understrength and not too well trained Militia – a force raised by compulsory ballot which, in principle, provided a system of universal national service but which, in practice, placed that obligation squarely on the shoulders of that large section of the population who had not the means to purchase exemption.

The Militia Ballot, although fair in principle, was ruined by a substitution system, which allowed a man who did not wish to render personal service to find a substitute, or to pay a fine to the Lieutenancy, which money then provided a bounty for a man to serve on his behalf. The scheme encouraged abuse, fostered corruption and placed an intolerable burden on the parish which was responsible for the maintenance of militiamen's families. When linked to the exemptions granted to members of the volunteer force, the system was in later years to have a drastic effect on the numbers and quality of the men available for service with the regular army. The immediate problem however, was the need to strengthen the land forces available to the government for home defence, and the Prime Minister, William Pitt, placed new proposals to remedy the problem before the House of Commons on 5 March, 1794. Shortly thereafter an Act [1] was passed which, in addition to including measures for strengthening the Militia, also authorised the raising, at comparatively little cost to government, of volunteer corps of all arms which could be used for both home defence and internal security. Clause 31 of the Act aimed "To encourage and discipline such Corps and Companies as should voluntarily enrol themselves for the defence of their counties, towns, coasts, or for the general defence of the Kingdom". Such corps, if accepted, who in the event of invasion or other emergency were caused to march on the King's service, would receive the same pay as regular troops and be subject to military discipline. The response to the call was considerable, and is described by Fortescue:

> There sprang up an infinity of Volunteer Corps, Infantry, Artillery, and Light Horse or Yeomanry Cavalry, first in single Companies and Troops, but very soon in Battalions and Regiments. [2]

The Act exempted Volunteers from service in the Militia, provided that such a man could could produce a certificate from his commanding officer to state that he had punctually attended the drills and exercises of his corps for at least six weeks prior to the hearing of appeals against the enforcement of the Militia Ballot. This loophole was as damaging to the principle of universal national service as was the substitution scheme allowed under the Militia Act. In consequence, not all of the men who came forward to serve as Volunteers were motivated by patriotism. Landowners and employers soon found Volunteer service to be a convenient method of protecting their best employees from the

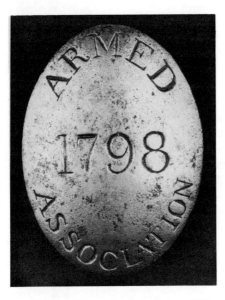

Cross belt plate, Armed Association, 1798.
National Museum of Wales:
Welsh Folk Museum

Militia Ballot and thereby safeguard their personal interests. The practice ensured that the Militia through ballot, did not get an 'across the board' selection of the manpower which was available; the force was compelled to draw from the numbers of those who remained unexempted. What remained was then available to the naval press gang or the regular army recruiter. Fortescue was later to state that the "dissociation of Volunteers from the Militia was a great and disastrous blunder." [3]

Particularly favoured by the government were the Corps of Yeomanry Cavalry, partly because of their mobility, and also because such corps consisted mainly of landowners and their tenant farmers. This strata of society, having roots in the land and being owners of property, had more to lose than most, and was consequently a useful arm to call upon in aid of the civil power. Having local knowledge they were also a most useful addition to the regular cavalry serving at home, as a strong mobile force was considered essential in the event of the French gaining a foothold on the coast. The enemy, it was reasoned, would in accordance with their custom, attempt to live off the land. That opportunity the cavalry would deny them by enforcing evacuation and a scorched earth policy. They would also harass the enemy flanks and lines of communication, thus forcing the them to fall back onto the coast. Compelled to supply their Army of England by sea, they would then be at the mercy of the Royal Navy and in consequence be starved into submission.

First in the field in Glamorgan was John Beavan's Corps of Swansea Volunteer Infantry which, by 1796, numbered three companies. Elsewhere in the county progress was slow with the movement not gaining much momentum until 1797-98 when, spurred into action by the then recent French landing in West Pembrokeshire, Volunteer units were raised with some rapidity. This first phase peaked in 1799, continued across the turn of the century to April 1802 when, following the return of peace, the majority of the part time soldiers were disembodied.

By May 1802, the Infantry Volunteers of Glamorgan had stood down leaving only the Swansea, Fairwood and Cardiff Troops of Yeomanry Cavalry in service, whose members having first elected to continue to serve on at their own expense, were shortly thereafter able to take advantage of new terms of service and financial assistance offered to them by the government under Act 42, Geo II, c 66.

At this stage attention must also be drawn to the Defence of the Realm Act of 1798 [4] which required the Lords Lieutenant to compile lists of all able-bodied men between the ages of 15 and 60, together with details of their occupation, and stipulating the type of service, combatant or non-combatant, which they would be capable of performing in times of emergency. The Act allowed the formation of Armed Associations, in which persons so registered in a community could unite to form bands of 50 men, primarily for local defence. The administration of such bodies was to be the responsibility of locally elected committees, and the officers would be selected by ballot of the local inhabitants. The essential difference between these associations and other volunteer corps was that the former were very localised in their activities and could also make use of the non-combatant element, namely men who, by reason of age or other cause, could not, or had no wish to bear arms. These men were made constables, reponsible for marshalling civilians, organising transport and herding livestock in the event of evacuation. Others were to become look-outs, beacon watchers and drivers of requisitioned waggons. Sadly many of the Associations raised in Wales were not listed in official records, but the few which have been traced appear to have been fairly rapidly absorbed into the ranks of larger Volunteer formations. The *Levee en Masse* lists associated with the Act can be of great value to the family historian. Such as have survived are mainly found in private, parish or borough records. To date, none have been found which relate to Glamorgan.

Pay was allowed to Volunteers who agreed to serve at any point within the Severn Military District - a day's exercise earned them the following rates:

Colonel	£1 2s 6d [£1.125]	
Lt Colonel	15s 11d	
Major	14s 1d	
Captain	9s 5d	
Ensign	3s 5d	
Adjutant	3s 9d	
Sergeants & Corporals	1s 0d	
Drummers & Privates	6d [2.5p]	

Weapons were supplied from government sources, and consisted of muskets with bayonets or pikes, or a mixture of both. Where government issues fell short of requirements it was not unusual for commanding officers to make good the shortfall by purchase from private sources. Other allowances were skimpy which resulted in the dress and appearance of a Volunteer unit depending greatly on the affluence of its officers and sponsors. Those with past military service tended to follow the styles of their old regiments, but highly popular was the style of dress worn by the red coated Light Infantry of the line or the dark green of the Rifles. Where funds were limited, second hand clothing was purchased from army contractors. As head-dress, the fur crested Tarleton helmet of the pattern worn by the Light Dragoons and Yeomanry Cavalry was greatly favoured. Others wore low crowned false-fronted Light Infantry caps or the more modest bicorne adorned with a worsted plume or coloured feather. Volunteers were quite often caricatured in the most unflattering terms, whereas in truth, many corps, both in turn out and drill, could compare favourably with the regular land forces. The type of man involved was, irrespective of motive, more often than not, far superior in both physique and intellect to the type of man serving as a private in the regular army. Unlike his regular army counterpart, the Volunteer was not subject to a harsh military discipline or ruled by the lash. Changing circumstances fortunately denied them the opportunity of proving themselves in battle, and in that respect their history is somewhat disadvantaged. Several opinions have been expressed regarding their usefulness in that situation, and not all are complimentary. It is my personal belief that, well led, they would have given a good account of themselves.

The Volunteers were at first extremely popular with the public, until the latter realised that such men could, in addition to defending their countrymen against the perils of invasion, also be used against them. Such situations arose when Volunteers honoured their obligation to act in aid of the civil power.

Notes
1. Act 34, Geo II, c31.
2. Fortescue, J W, *History of the British Army*
3. Ibid.
4. Act 38. Geo II, c18, c19 and c27.

Chapter 4
THE VOLUNTEER CORPS, 1796-1802

Swansea Royal Volunteers
Raised in 1796 and commanded by Captain John Beavan, the corps role was specifically the defence of the town of Swansea. The use of the term 'Royal' in its title suggests high patronage, but no evidence has been found to support such a

connection. The term 'Loyal' was more commonplace in Volunteer corps titles of the period, and more descriptive of the patriotic feeling which led to their creation. Other officers serving in the Corps were:

Captain William Jones
Captain John Landeg
Captain Lieutenant J W Mansfield
Lt John Tucker
Lt and Surgeon John Roberts
Ensign Rees Jones
Ensign John Williams
Ensign John Bowen Adjutant and Quartermaster [1]

The number of captains suggests a corps of three companies, each of which numbered approximately 60 men. In March 1797, John Beavan is listed as a Lt Colonel and William Jones as Major, promotions which indicate an increase in the strength of the corps to at least four or more companies.[2] By April 1797, John Landeg had succeeded Beavan as Lt Colonel Commandant. Other officers at that date were:

Major William Jones
Captain John W Mansfield
Captain David Long
Captain Lieutenant John Tucker
Lt David Davies
Lt Rees Jones
Lt John Bowen
Ensign John Grove
Ensign John Williams
Ensign William Phillips
Quartermaster David Hopkins [3]

E H Stuart Jones in his book *The Last Invasion of Britain* tells us that part of the 180 strong corps was in February 1797 called out to check, what transpired to be a false report, of a French landing at Rhossili.

The corps was not one of those absorbed by the Swansea Legion on its formation in July 1800, but remained independent until its disbandment in 1802.

No details of any colours which may have been carried have been found, nor any description of the uniform dress.

Cowbridge Volunteer Infantry

Raised by John Beavan, Esq, the Cowbridge Volunteer Infantry was accepted for service in March 1797, the Cowbridge Corporation subscribing the sum of £20 to assist with the expenses. A list of May 1797 shows two officers with commissions dated 23 March, 1797 – Captain Commandant John Beavan and Lt Thomas Williams. Later, two Ensigns were appointed - Francis Baynton (4 July, 1798) and Edward Nichol (24 October, 1799).

25

From an original strength of one company, the corps had by 1801 expanded to three, by which date John Beavan is listed as its Major Commandant.

No information has been found regarding the dress of this corps, but like most others of the kind, the style was probably not dissimilar to that worn by the line infantry of the period. A Colour was presented to the corps about November 1797.

> The Cowbridge Independent Volunteers were presented with Colours on Friday last at a grand Field Day. The Standard was a present from a young lady, a perfect stranger in the County. It is printed in an elegant manner on white silk. On one side the Cowbridge Arms over the Arms of Glamorgan, the first encircled with the Welsh Motto - 'EIN DUW, EIN GWLAD, EIN BRENIN' [Our God, Our Country, Our King], ornamented with supports in gold and scarlet on which hang festoons of laurel foliage in green and silver. On the other side the letters C V, in a cipher of green and gold on an azure ground, over which a beautiful plume of Ostrich feathers, very appropriate to them as a Welsh Corps. The Motto and foliage the same as on the other side. The Colours were consecrated by the Rev Williams, Master of the Grammar School. [4]

The Arms of Cowbridge are described as 'patred chevronwise gules and argent, the chief strewn with silver crossletts, and amongst them two lions rampant argent, and in the base a cow passant on a bridge over water, all proper'. The description suggests that the designs described were printed, as opposed to being embroidered on the silk, and that the ostrich plumes depicted the badge of the Prince of Wales. Sadly no record of what became of the colour has been found, or of any suggestion that it was laid up locally.

A series of verses in praise of the Cowbridge Volunteers was written by Edward Williams (Iolo Morgannwg) and were sung to the tune known as *Batchelors All*. [5]

> While War pours around all its terrible storms
> And danger appears in numberless forms,
> We, mid the wild uproar that spreads its alarms
> Volunteered for our Country, fly boldly to arms,
> At Liberty's call, every soul is awake,
> We the field to crush tyranny cheerfully take,
> And oppose the sharp steel, and the death pinioned ball,
> To the barbarous foes that would Britons enthral.
>
> *Chorus*
> *One and all, one and all, all Liberty call,*
> *To vanquish the foes that would Britons enthral*
>
> We Son's of Glamorgan, of Britain's old race,
> Eye with filial affection our dear native place,
> No Nation before us this religion possess'd,
> To this day, tis our own, in its plenty we're blessed,

The Saxon, the Dane and the Norman in vain,
Strove to bind our forefather's in tyranny's chain
And if we one moment experienced a fall,
Soon we sprang from the grasp that would Britons enthrall.

Iolo continues this patriotic outpouring for another five verses, which effort to those aware of his previous political leanings must have come across as a blatant piece of hypocrisy. He was well known for his earlier support of the French revolutionary cause, and had at the outbreak of that bloodbath, described it as "The dawn of the day of our Liberty". His outburt in praise of the patriots of Cowbridge was in complete contrast to some of his earlier concoctions, amongst the most notorious of which were probably *The Newgate Stanzas* and his famous *Song on the Rights of Man* written in 1793. Amongst the enemies of liberty which he attacked at that stage were "Kings and Priests", and he was quite categoric in declaring that France was the only country where the "Rights of Man" were enthroned. He was fortunate at that time in not ending up as a 'Guest of His Majesty', and it was probably fear of that consequence which led to the sudden dampening of the old rogue's revolutionary ardour.

The Cowbridge Corps, in company with other Glamorgan Infantry Volunteers, stood down in 1802.

Neath Gentlemen and Yeomanry

Raised by Captain John Nathaniel Miers, the services of the Neath Gentlemen and Yeomanry Cavalry were accepted in May 1797. Other officers appointed were Lt John Morgan and Cornet Lewis Jenkins, whose commissions, including that of Captain Miers were dated May 3 1797. Two further appointments were made on May 31 1798, when Thomas Leyson was appointed Adjutant and Samuel Freeman as Cornet, vice Jenkins.

No information has been found concerning the style of dress worn, but it was undoubtedly of a style and pattern similar to that worn by other Glamorgan Yeomanry Cavalry units of that period.

This single troop of about 40 men served through until the general disembodiment of Glamorgan Volunteers

A drawing of a Tarleton helmet badge worn by an unidentified Glamorgan Infantry Volunteer corps, c1800. A badge of this pattern was offered for sale at the Wallis & Wallis Sale-rooms, c1970.

27

in April 1802, but for reasons not known, it did not take advantage of the opportunity given to such mounted units to continue in service. Had it done so, it would have ranked as the senior troop of the later consolidated Corps of Glamorgan Yeomanry Cavalry.

Bridgend Volunteer Infantry

Accepted for service in May 1797, its original officers were:

Captain John Bennett
Lt John Pritchard
Lt Joseph May
Ensign Llewelyn

All the commissions, with the exception of Llewelyn's, are dated May 22 1797, with Llewelyn appointed later on June 1. By July 1797, Henry Knight of Tythegston had been appointed Major Commandant, and the corps strength increased from one to three companies. Additional officers appointed to cover were – Captain John Richardson and Lt Daniel Jones (26 July 1797), Ensign Richard Burnell and Ensign John Williams (16 August 1797).

The *Hereford Journal* of the period contains several references to this Volunteer corps as, for example in 1801, when Henry Knight's promotion to Lieutenant Colonel is reported. That promotion indicates a further increase in the strength of the corps to possibly 4 or 5 companies. The Bridgend Volunteer Infantry stood down in April 1802.

No information has been found concerning uniform dress.

The Swansea Gentlemen and Yeomanry

Included in the Bute Lieutenancy Papers is a proposal submitted to the Glamorgan Quarter Sessions in 1792 by a certain unnamed gentleman in West Glamorgan offering to raise an Armed Association of mounted volunteers for the protection of the coast, and if called upon, to also act in aid of the civil power. [6]

Whereas the County of Glamorgan from its maritime situation is exposed to danger from the enemy in time of War, the inhabitants having been frequently alarmed by French Privateers cruising in the Bristol Channel, hovering near the coast, and even anchoring in the Mumbles Road, and whereas great depredations have been made on the larger of the ships stranded on the coast for want of proper assistance, and whereas the speedy assembly of a Body of Armed Men of Property in the County would in all these cases tend to the safety and protection of the Publick and to the protection of the property of individuals, and whereas the institution of a respectable Constitutional Force would strike terror into the minds of evil disposed persons, so as to prevent probably the mischiefs that arise from the misguided and ignorant Bodies of People being misled for the purpose of plundering Ships or other wicked intentions, and whereas no sufficient assistance can be had from the Civil Power of the County by the ordinary sense of Law in such extraordinary cases or sudden emergencies, nor the necessary assistance speedily collected when most wanted, unless prepared by some previous arrangement with the proper Arms and Number; We, whose names are here underwritten, Do, for the purpose aforesaid, and at all times to preserve the Publick Peace of the County, agree to Associate ourselves as a body to act in conjunction upon all occasions, and to provide ourselves severally with a Blue Coat of one uniform make and colour, a white Waistcoat and Breeches by way of distinction and regularity, and also one pair of Horse Pistols and a Cutlass with Belts and a Pouch for Powder and Ball, and to be prepared with a Horse to mount on any summons for the purpose expressed, and we do further agree to associate ourselves and to be known by the name of The Protecting Fellowship, and do elect and nominate to be our Chief Man and Leader ————.

This proposal, as far as can be determined, was the first attempt made to raise the equivalent of a troop of Yeomanry Cavalry in the county. The move does not appear to have been any more successful than the later attempt, made about 1797, which proposal is contained in a memorandum in the same series of Lieutenancy documents, part of which reads:

1. That this Troop serve without pay as a local Independent Corps during the War and within the County of Glamorgan, and for the defence of the Town and neighbourhood of Swansea, subject in that situation to the Orders of the General or Senior Officer Commanding the District.

2. That they will provide themselves with Horses and Clothing.

3. The Officers to consist of one Captain, one Lieutenant and one Cornet.

4. That the above proposals be transmitted to the Lord Lieutenant requesting him, should he approve of same, to submit them to His Majesty.

The memorandum is interesting in that it exemplifies the basic terms of service for many Volunteer corps. The key figure in each case was the Lord Lieutenant as, without his approval, no Volunteer unit could be accepted. In respect of Yeomanry Cavalry, the requirement that each man provide at his own expense, a horse and his uniform clothing, determined the class of men from which such units could be raised.

On May 1st, 1797, the *Gloucester Journal* listed the following gentlemen as officers of the Swansea Cavalry:

Captain John Llewelyn of Penllergaer
Lt Ralph Sheldon
Cornet John Jones

John Llewelyn also appears in the Army List of that year as Captain of the Troop – gazetted 27 April, but for reasons unexplained, matters do not appear to have progressed any further, as plans for raising a troop of Volunteer cavalry in

Swansea were still under discussion in May 1798. On 3 May of that year, the proposal was again accepted, and two officers were appointed – Captain Thomas Morgan (a local lawyer and agent for the Duke of Beaufort in that district), with Thomas Hughes as his Lieutenant. Just under a year later, John Mills was appointed Cornet.

No mention is made of the officers appointed in 1797 – presumably they became tired of waiting and withdrew. John Llewelyn in the meantime had continued his interest, but diverted it into raising a corps of volunteer infantry styled the Glamorgan Rangers. The troop numbering 40-50 men was trained by one Robert Hale, presumably a retired NCO of the regular cavalry. A receipt in the Bute Papers shows that he devoted thirteen weeks to the task and also includes his scale of charges.

> Received 3rd November, 1798, of Thomas Morgan, Esq, the Sum of Sixteen Pounds, Five Shillings, being for thirteen weeks attendance in drilling a Troop of Horse at the Rate of £1. 5. 0 per week, which settles the annex'd Bill.

In April 1800, the troop was called out in aid of the civil power when corn riots broke out in Neath and Swansea. Fortunately, the Yeomen were not called upon to exercise force, as their arrival on the scene was sufficient to persuade the discontented to disperse.

On 25 July 1800, the War Office sanctioned the formation of an armed body to be known as the Swansea Legion, which was to be created from an amalgamation of the volunteer cavalry and infantry corps already active in the district.

Command of the Legion was given to Lt Colonel Thomas Morgan, who in taking over the new responsibility, handed over the command of the Swansea troop to Captain Edward Hughes. Between that date and April 1802, the corps was also referred to as the Swansea Legion Cavalry. In April 1802, the infantry element of the Swansea Legion stood down and the Legion ceased to exist. The Swansea Troop of Yeomanry Cavalry continued in service, taking advantage of an Act which allowed them to do so, but more will be said on that score later.

The uniform dress worn by the Swansea troop on formation was similar in most respects to that worn by the regular Light Dragoons of the day. The head-dress consisted of the Light Dragoon pattern or Tarleton helmet made of leather and decorated with a large bearskin crest. From invoices held in the Bute Papers we are able to establish that it had a leopard skin turban wound around the leather headpiece which was secured with gilded chain. The helmet described was very likely that worn by an officer and was priced at £2 1s 6d [£2.07]. It had gilded fittings and was decorated with a white feather hackle on the left hand side. Another invoice prices a Tarleton helmet at £1, probably second hand stock for the use of the troopers. Above the peak was a metal strip stamped with the title

GLAMORGAN YEO'N CAVALRY. At a later date, but probably not before 1803, silver or white metal fittings replaced the gilt.

Another invoice lists a farrier's cap complete with horseshoe badge at 16 shillings. No detailed description of the cap is given but Captain Hinde in his *Discipline of the Light Horse* (1778) states that the "Farriers wear black bearskin Caps with a Horseshoe in front". Another work of reference [7] describes farriers as wearing "a sort of Grenadier Cap with a fur front". Presumably the cap worn by the farrier of the Swansea Troop was of similar description. The same invoice lists a trumpeters cap at £1 5s 0d [£1.25]. No description is given, but a Commander-in-Chief's Circular dated March 1792 states that "trumpeters of all Regiments of Light Dragoons are for the future to wear black bearkin Caps instead of Hats as before ordered ". Again, one can only assume that the Swansea Cavalry conformed with that instruction.

A letter in the Bute Papers dated 23 June, 1793, tells us that the hip length scarlet jacket worn by the Swansea Troop was turned back with black velvet and was worn over a white waistcoat. The jacket had gilded buttons which carried as a motif the plumes, coronet and motto of the Prince of Wales positioned over the letters 'S V C'. White leather or white kerseymere breeches worn with black knee length military boots completed the outfit. All ranks wore a pipeclayed leather crossbelt which supported a black leather ammunition pouch, white leather swordbelts and slings which supported a regulation pattern Light Cavalry sabre in its polished steel scabbard.

The troop carried a black silk standard (or guidon) with an armorial design. The standard was supplied by Thomas Hawkins, 'Cap Makers to their Majesties' and cost £1 8s 0d. It is likely that the armorial design was a combination of the crest of the Prince of Wales and the arms of Swansea.

The Fairwood Troop of Gentlemen and Yeomanry

Raised in 1798 by Captain Sir Gabriel Powell, very little is known of the activities of this unit during the period 1798-1802.

On being raised it consisted of a Captain Commandant (Sir Gabriel Powell), one lieutenant, one cornet and between 30-50 yeomen, and operated in a local defence role on the Gower Peninsula. It did not unite with the Swansea Cavalry and other volunteer corps to form part of the Swansea Legion, but remained independent. In 1802, it followed the example of the Swansea and Cardiff troops by continuing in service at members expense, but later took advantage of the new government offer to remain in service.

Gabriel Powell's commission was dated 27th June 1798, which date can be taken as the starting point for this corps.

Its style of dress was similar to the Swansea Troop except that the scarlet jacket carried yellow facings and was embellished with silver lace.

The Cardiff Troop of Gentlemen and Yeomanry

Raised in 1798, the chief organiser of this corps of 47 yeomen was William Vaughan who was gazetted as its Captain Commandant on the 26 June 1798. Later, in February 1800, John Wood, Esq, was appointed as 1st Lieutenant. The corps was trained by an ex-NCO of the 18th Light Dragoons and its activities were mainly concerned with the local defence of Cardiff. One local historian in a history of Cardiff, incorrectly states that in 1799 the troop was inspected by its "Commanding Officer, Colonel Awbrey". Although very likely inspected by the good Colonel, it should be noted that Awbrey was at the time Commanding Officer of the Glamorgan Regiment of Militia and had no connection whatsoever with the Yeomanry Cavalry.

On 25 October, 1799, John Perkins, a farmer of Llantrithyd, recorded in his diary [8] that he watched the troop at exercise with the Cowbridge Infantry Volunteers in a field called *Tynakaia* (possibly Ty'n y Caeau).

In September 1800, when called out in aid of the civil power, the troop marched to Merthyr Tydfil, where it successfully dispersed a large crowd of discontented workers in the vicinity of the Castle Inn. Its members later searched out and arrested the ringleaders of the unrest and escorted them to Cardiff to stand trial.

The troop continued in service at its own expense following the general disembodiment of Glamorgan Volunteers in April 1802, but was later able to take advantage of new government terms to remain in service.

The dress of the Cardiff troop was similar to that worn by the Fairwood troop of Yeomanry Cavalry.

Neath Infantry Volunteers

Raised by Henry Smith Thomas, Esq, the Neath Infantry Volunteers were accepted for service in June, 1798 when its officers were Captain Henry Smith Thomas, Lt John Child and Ensign Solomon Bowen whose Commissions were dated 6 June 1798. Listed also, but without a date for his commission was Ensign Thomas Glasson. [9]

At first the corps consisted of one company, but was increased by 1801 to three. In that year Henry Smith Thomas is listed as Major Commandant. The corps stood down in April 1802.

Glamorgan Rangers Volunteers

Prime movers in raising this unit were Thomas Mansel Talbot of Margam Abbey and John Llewelyn of Penllergaer. The Rangers were the largest independent corps in the county and had companies active in an area extending from Penllergaer in the west to Margam and Maesteg in the east. Accepted for service by August 1798, its officers in that month were:

Lt Colonel Commandant Thomas Mansel Talbot
Lt Colonel John Llewelyn
Major Calvert Richard Jones
Captain John Morris
Captain John Lucas
Captain Thomas Lockwood
Captain Charles Smith
Captain Lieutenant Edward King
1st Lt James Brogden of Tondu
1st Lt Allen Page
1st Lt George Harris
1st Lt Illtyd Thomas of Glanmor
1st Lt Thomas Morris
2nd Lt Francis Beavan
2ndLt John Minshall
2nd Lt John Charles Collins
2nd Lt Thomas Potts
2nd Lt John Jeffrey
2nd Lt Thomas Watkins.
Chaplain Rev Thomas Powell. [10]

The corps consisted of at least five companies and numbered approximately 250-300 volunteers.

The term 'Rangers' invariably described a Rifles Corps and consequently the uniform dress worn was almost certainly rifle green with black or scarlet facings and with black leather accoutrements. No documentary or other evidence has been found to support this premise.

In 1902, the Rev J D Davies, Rector of Cheriton in the Gower, obtained from one of his parishoners, a Mr John Chalk of Cheriton Glebe, the words of an old song which he had often heard his late father sing.

Colonel Talbot leads the van,
Bless the County, skilful man,
Twas he who formed that wondrous plan
Of the old Glamorgan Rangers.

Captain Gordon bold and free,
A better man could never be,
We'll follow him o'er land and sea
Say the old Glamorgan Rangers.

There were probably other verses, but sadly Mr Chalk could only remember two, which were duly recorded in the parish magazine.

As far as is known, there exists only one item which was associated with the corps, namely a brass shoulder belt plate which once formed part of the author's collection. The oval brass plate which bears traces of gilding and has superimposed on its face, the numeral '3' above a bugle horn, plain and without

Shoulder belt plate, Glamorgan Volunteer Rangers, c1799. [Welch Regiment Museum]

strings. Engraved around the lower edge of the plate is the title *GLAMORGAN VOLUNTEER RANGERS*. The numeral '3', presumably refers to the third company of the corps. The Glamorgan Rangers stood down during the general disembodiment of the county volunteers in April, 1802.

Swansea Volunteer Artillery

Raised and commanded by Captain Stephen Jones in 1798, as far as is known this unit had the distinction of being the only Volunteer artillery unit active in the county. No dates have been found for the commissions of Captain Jones or his Lieutenant, Stephen Prance, Esq.

The Bute MSS refer to a proposal to amalgamate the corps with the Oystermouth Volunteer Infantry, but do not state whether or not the unification took place. It is possible that the corps became part of the Swansea Legion in 1800, as that body was known to be in possession of one or two artillery pieces.

The corps does not appear to have continued in service after the general disembodiment of 1802.

Oystermouth Volunteer Infantry

That such a unit existed is confirmed by press reports and the Bute Lieutenancy Papers, but no record of its activities have been found. It is my opinion that it evolved from an Armed Association known as the Swansea Volunteer Association raised by Captain Samuel Hancorne in 1798. It is not listed as one of the local corps which united to form the Swansea Legion in 1800. There is no record of it continuing in service after April 1802.

Lougher Infantry Volunteers

Also known as the Gower and Lougher Volunteers, this corps was raised in 1798 by William Augustus Pengree of Lougher who was in due course appointed its Captain Commandant. The other officers were Lt Thomas Mathews and Ensign Henry Pengree, whose commissions, like that of their Captain, were dated 27 June, 1798.

The Bute Papers tell us that in addition to the officers listed that the corps, consisting of one company, united with others to form the Swansea Legion in July 1800.

Llangyfelach Infantry Volunteers

Raised by Roger Landeg, its Captain Commandant, this corps, consisting of one company, came into existance about June or July 1798. Other officers were Lt Thomas Jones and Ensign Thomas Jones whose appointments were publicised in the press, but were undated. [11]

The corps are recorded as being clothed in red jackets of a pattern similar to those worn by the Line infantry of the day.

It united with others to form the Swansea Legion in July 1800.

Caerphilly Volunteer Infantry

Raised by Captain William Williams, the corps, originally two companies strong, was accepted for service in June 1798. With commissions dated 27 June its officers were:

Captain William Williams
Lt James Jacobs
Lt David Edwards
Ensign Thomas Kingsbury
Ensign David Williams

On 29 August, 1798, Major William Goodrich was appointed Major Commandant of the corps which at that date numbered three companies. Additional officers appointed on 27 August were :

Captain Richard Rice Williams
Lt Thomas Morgan Bassett
Ensign Rowland Williams

The corps wore a red coat similar to that worn by the line infantry and, if the backcloth of the Regimental Colour can be taken as guide, blue facings.

In 1800, the Caerphilly Volunteers were drawn out in readiness to proceed to Merthyr Tydfil where rioting had taken place but, due to the arrival of regular cavalry in that district, their services were fortunately not required. The corps stood down and was disbanded in April 1802.

Colours were presented to the corps by the Marchioness of Bute and John Goodrich, Esq, of Energlyn – the father of the Commanding Officer. These colours survived to pass into the hands of the Commanding Officer, 2nd Welsh Brigade, Royal Field Artillery (TA) in 1920 in the mistaken belief that the Caerphilly Battery of the Brigade were the lineal successors of the 18th century Caerphilly Volunteer Corps. It is fortunate that some years later the military saw

Top: King's Colour, Caerphilly Infantry Volunteers, c1800.
Bottom: Regimental Colour, Caerphilly Infantry Volunteers, c1800.
[National Museum of Wales: Welsh Folk Museum]

fit to hand the colours over to the National Museum of Wales for preservation and safe keeping. For many years they hung in a prominent position in the main entrance hall of that establishment, but in the 1970s they were taken down and removed to the Welsh Folk Museum at St Fagan's in the interests of long term conservation.

The King's Colour – Dimensions 6' x 6' 6"– a Great Union of the pre-1801 pattern (without the Cross of St Patrick). At its centre, the arms of the Bute family, above which, a scroll inscribed *LOYAL VOLUNTEERS CAERPHILLY HUNDRED*. Below the Bute arms, another scroll inscribed *GIFT OF THE MARCHIONESS OF BUTE* astride the Union wreath.

The Regimental Colour – Dimensions 6' x 6' 6" – a blue silk colour with the pre-1801 Union Flag in the top canton. At the centre, an oval enclosure bounded by the Union wreath, inside of which is depicted a view of Caerphilly Castle. Above and astride the Union wreath, a Scroll inscribed *LOYAL VOLUNTEERS CAERPHILLY HUNDRED*. Below the castle and astride the wreath, there is another scroll inscribed *THE GIFT OF JOHN GOODRICH, ESQ*.

Loyal Gower Volunteer Association

Raised by Robert Hancorne, who was also its Captain, the Association was formed about July or August 1798. No further information apart from a brief note in the *Hereford Journal* has been found. It is my personal belief that this small Association was absorbed into the Loyal Independent Gower Volunteers in January 1799.

Pennard and Oystermouth Loyal Association

The Bute Papers in October 1798 refer to this Armed Association, but no record of its existence has been found elsewhere. Its officers were Captain Edward Shewen and Lt William Grove. In view of Edward Shewen's later connection with the Loyal Independent Gower Infantry Volunteers, it is my opinion that this Association in 1799 provided the nucleus for the larger corps and in consequence underwent a change of title.

Loyal Independent Gower Volunteers

Raised by Edward Shewen, Esq, this corps of infantry volunteers was accepted for service in January 1799. Its officers whose commissions were dated 17 January were Captain Edward W Shewen, Lt David Bevan and Ensign William Green.

The Bute Papers contain an invoice (which relates to this corps) from William Prater and Company, London, addressed to Captain Shewen and lists the following items:

Gorget, Loyal Gower Infantry Volunteers. [Dr J Carey Hughes]

57 Light Infantry Jackets and Waistcoats
3 Sergeants Light Infantry Jackets and Waistcoats
2 Yards of Gold Fringe
6 Yards of Gold Lace
2 Drummers Jackets and Yellow Waistcoats
3 Corporals Epaulettes

From that information one deduces that the corps consisted of one company comprising 3 officers, 3 sergeants, 3 corporals, 2 drummers and 57 privates, who were dressed in the fashion of the Light Infantry of the line.

There exists in a private collection an example of the gorget worn by officers of this corps. Gilt on copper, it has engraved on its face the intertwined letters 'LGV' set within an open ended wreath of laurel leaves. Approximate dimensions being 110 x 105mm. In July 1800, the corps was united with others to form the Swansea Legion Infantry.

Merthyr Tydfil Infantry Volunteers

E H Stuart Jones in his Book *The Last Invasion of Britain* states that Richard Crawshay of Cyfarthfa, on hearing of the French landing near Fishguard in February 1797, hurriedly enrolled one thousand of his workmen, and having armed them with pikes produced in his iron foundry, prepared to march them to the scene of action. News of the French surrender made the journey unnecessary, at which stage the armed workforce presumably stood down. Almost three years were to pass before the Volunteer movement got off the ground officially in the town, at some date in late 1799 or early 1800.

A *History of Merthyr Tydfil* [12] lists three officers – Captain Watkin George of Cyfarthfa, Captain Williams (a local lawyer) and Captain Meyrick which appointments suggest a corps of three companies.

In fine weather the corps drilled in a field at the back of buildings known as Coffin's Houses in Georgetown and, in inclement weather, in the Old Casting House at Ynysfach.

A poem in honour of the corps was written by William Moses (Gwilym Tew) and was titled *Gwroldeb Milwyr Cartrefol Merthyr* [The Bravery of the Local Soldiers of Merthyr].

Charles Williams, in his *History of Merthyr Tydfil* makes reference to the corps, but suggests that it was not raised until 1800.

> Early in 1800 the Ironmasters had held a consultation on the subject of enrolment and the result was immediately shown by the raising of three Companies commanded by Captain Watkin George.

The corps had a Drill Sergeant, surname Wynne (or Wynn), engaged by the ironmasters of Cyfarthfa but, due to the fact that he spoke no Welsh, he found great difficulty in imparting his military knowledge to the volunteers – a problem quite widespread, particularly amongst the Welsh militia regiments of the period.

Williams goes on to describe the uniform dress as being "Red jackets with yellow facings the same as the Regiments of the Line".

> White trousers in the summer and dark for the winter were supplied, with a bullet pouch, dry and oiled rag, pipe clay, and with a common musket which merited the name White Bess. Its polished barrel was not approved of, and a descendant of the Merthyr Volunteers remembers his worthy Sire hearing an Officer at Swansea strongly condemn them as liable to burst. "

The volunteers were drawn mainly from the labourers of the iron works, the trades section being only feebly represented. It would appear that some element of compulsion existed, but the reason behind that can hardly have been a desire to protect their most valued employees from the demands of the Militia Ballot.

The men drilled daily, receiving 13 pence for their efforts. When on Permanent Duty in Swansea or Cardiff they received 2 shillings and 6 pence (12$\frac{1}{2}$p). A bugle called summoned the volunteers for daily drill which commenced at 10am, when Wynne kept them hard at it until 1pm. Afterwards they were allowed to report for normal work. Latecomers or absentees were punished with extra drill, and if persistant risked being dismissed from their employment. The historian Wilkins describes Sergeant Wynne as a bit of a military showman; the worthy sergeant combining his duties as instructor with that of recruiter for the Army. His headquarters for the latter duty was most appropriately, an inn known as the King's Arms.

The Drill Master and chief Military Factotum was Sergeant Wynne, a fine fellow, who had seen service abroad, and continuously wore a battered breastplate which had once turned a Musket Ball from his heart.

It is likely that the breastplate was a recruiting gimmick aimed at impressing young men, and persuading them in due course to accept a free drink and thence the 'King's Shilling'.

Although I have quoted from Williams' history in discussing this unit some of his statements lead me to believe that he is at times referring to the contribution made by the town to the East Glamorgan Infantry post 1803. The Merthyr Tydfil corps stood down in 1802 and were disbanded.

Aberdare Infantry Volunteers

An infantry Volunteer corps commanded by Captain Tom Rees of Werfa was active in Aberdare about 1800. No trace of them can be found in any official list, but their existence is confirmed by Williams in his *History of Merthyr Tydfil*. Penrheolcerrig provided a place of exercise for them, quite often in association with the Merthyr Tydfil unit.

Kilvey Infantry Volunteers

A Volunteer corps of this name is listed in the Bute Papers as being one of the units which became part of the Swansea Legion in July 1800. Its name does not appear in any official list, and no mention of it has been found in the newspapers of that period.

Dowlais Infantry Volunteers

Although no record of this corps has been found in any official document, the existence of a Marksmanship Medal to Volunteer John Evans confirms that a corps of Volunteers was raised, probably from amongst the work force of the Dowlais Iron Works.

The Swansea Legion

On 25 July 1800, Captain Thomas Morgan of the Swansea Volunteer Cavalry, having handed over the command of that unit to Captain Edward Hughes, took up his new appointment as Lt Colonel Commandant of the Swansea Legion.

The Legion consisted of the following Swansea and district volunteer corps who, by common consent, had decided that more could be achieved in the event of emergency by acting as one large force under one commanding officer.

1 Troop of Swansea Volunteer Cavalry
1 Company of Lougher Volunteer Infantry - Captain Pengree
1 Company of Llangyfelach Volunteer Infantry - Captain R Landeg

40

Marksmanship Medal (obverse & reverse), Dowlais Infantry Volunteers, 1802.
[J L Balmer, TD]

1 Company Loyal Independent Gower Volunteers - Captain Shewen
1 Company Kilvey Volunteer Infantry

The stand down of the Glamorgan Volunteers in April 1802, saw the infantry of the Legion disbanded, but the Cavalry troop remained in service at its own expense and later applied to take advantage of new terms of service which were offered by government. Their offer of continued service as the Swansea Troop of Yeomanry Cavalry was accepted by the King on 31 August, 1802.

Notes
1. *Hereford Journal*, 16 November, 1796.
2. *Gloucester Journal*, 27 March, 1797.
3. *Hereford Jornal*, 5 April, 1797.
4. Ibid, 8 November, 1797.
5. *Men of Harlech*, Regimental Journal, Welch Regt, Vol III, No 9, 1895.
6. Bute Papers.
7. Lawson, C P, *History of the Regts and Uniforms of the British Army.*
8. Perkins Diary, Welsh Folk Museum, Farming & Rural Life Collection
9. *Hereford Journal*, 13 June, 1798
10. Ibid, 22 August, 1798
11. Ibid, 1 August, 1798
12. Wilkins, *A History of Merthyr Tydfil.*

Chapter 5
THE SHORT LIVED PEACE
MARCH 1802 TO MAY 1803

In March 1802 Addington's government agreed terms with the French under the Treaty of Amiens – a peace of sorts which did no more than allow a short breathing space for both sides.

The embodied regiments of Militia returned to their home counties and were disembodied and instructions were given for the Volunteers to stand down. By May 1802 the only Volunteer corps remaining in service in Glamorgan were the Swansea, Fairwood and Cardiff Troops of Yeomanry Cavalry, who had decided to continue to serve on at their own expense. The government recognising the value of such corps as an aid to civil power came forward in July with a circular letter to the Lords Lieutenant inviting offers of service from Volunteer corps not wishing to stand down. Nationally, a fair number of Volunteers both cavalry and infantry accepted the terms. but in Glamorgan, only the three Corps of Yeomanry already mentioned came forward, and their offer of continued service was accepted on 31 August 1802.

Members of units accepted for continued service were exempted from the Militia Ballot provided they attended the drills of their corps on five days in every year – a privilege forfeited should they for some reason be, or seek to be, discharged. They were entitled to relief from the duty on hair powder, and also on one horse. If they consented to march out of their county to repel invasion or in aid of civil power. they would receive the same pay as regular troops but be subject to military discipline. In the event of being subjected to a court martial, they could be tried by their own officers, and if disabled on service would be entitled to a Chelsea pension. Additionally, the following allowances were offered:

£2 per annum to every Volunteer for his Clothing and Appointments.
£60 per annum for every Troop of Horse numbering not less than 40 Rank and File.

Meanwhile, the weapons on issue to the disbanded volunteer units of Glamorgan infantry were ordered to be returned to the Militia Armoury in Cardiff for onward transmission to the Tower of London – a somewhat pointless exercise, as by the end of the year, it was clear that a renewal of hostilities was inevitable.

On 11 March 1803, in preparation for the conflict, an embodiment of Militia was ordered. On the 16 May, Great Britain and France were again at war.

Chapter 6
THE VOLUNTEER MOVEMENT, 1803-08

The measures taken to embody the Militia on March 11th 1803, were followed on 31 March by a call to the Lords Lieutenant to encourage the formation of volunteer units under terms offered by the Volunteer Act of 1802 [1]. The circular letter gave details of the composition of Volunteer corps and explained the terms of service:

> The Companies not to be less than 2 Sergeants, 2 Corporals, one Drummer and fifty Privates, each with one Captain, one Lieutenant, one Ensign. Two Lieutenants to the Flank Companies [2] , and to such as consist of eighty men; no Company to have more than one hundred Private Men.

Where a unit was large enough to merit the appointment of a field officer, the scale of appointment was to be similar to that already in force in the Militia. Adjutants and Sergeant Majors, on basic scales of pay similar to that allowed to the Permanent Staff of disembodied regiments of Militia, could be appointed to corps numbering 300 men. Effective Volunteers received training pay at the undermentioned rates for two days in the week from Lady Day to Michaelmas, and for one day of muster in each month when present and under arms.

> Sergeant 1/6
> Corporal 1/2
> Drummer 1/-
> Private 1/-

To be allowed for clothing:

> £3-3-9 for each sergeant
> £1-11-3 for each corporal
> £2-3-6 for each drummer
> £1-10-0 for each private

> An Annual Allowance to be made to each Company in lieu of all contingencies exclusive of agency; for each business a General Agent will be appointed by Government, Viz:- £25 for Companies of 50 Private Men, with an additional allowance of £5 for every 10 men beyond that number . . .

Field Officers and Adjutants to be allowed a Tax for one Horse each; the whole of the Officers and Men to be exempted from Hair Powder Duty and from being balloted for the Militia during their service in the Volunteers. [3]

This system of payment was termed the 'June Allowances' and units serving under the terms were allowed pay for up to 85 days exercise in any one year, in return for which they undertook to serve if required in any part of the military district [4]. Some short time later the Army Reserve Act [5] and *Levee en Masse* Act [6] encouraged the formation of even more volunteer units, a clause from the Army Reserve Act stipulating that exemption from the Militia ballot could only be granted to a volunteer provided his name appeared on the Muster Roll of a corps before 22 June, 1803. To cope with the additional numbers, and in order to minimise expenditure, the government agreed to provide Volunteer units accepted after 22 June with pay for only 20 days training in any one year, which system was termed the 'August Allowances'. Such corps had to agree to march to any part of Great Britain in the event of invasion or of the appearance in force of any enemy off the coast, and also to assist the civil power in the suppression of any rebellion or insurrection existing or which might arise at the time of the emergency.[7] On the 31 August 1803, the government accepted the offers of service of all the Volunteer corps which had been submitted, but stipulated that any man over and above a figure equal to six times the County Militia Regiment quota would have to be classed as a supernumary, and as such, would not be entitled to allowances or exemptions of any kind.[8] The Militia quota for Glamorgan was at the time 403 private men, hence the total number of Volunteers allowed amounted to 2,418. Scope for expanding the Volunteer force in time of emergency was allowed by an arrangement which allowed the King in such circumstances to augment the various county Volunteer establishments by one half. Meanwhile, in the county, the Lord Lieutenant fixed the numerical strength which could be allowed. In Glamorgan, the newspapers closely followed all the developments:

The patriotism of the County of Glamorgan has not been exceeded by that of any County in the Kingdom. When invasion threatened, upwards of 4,700 of her gallant Sons volunteered their services to repel the insolent foe, of which 2,519 were accepted and are now embodied. [9]

Exactly how many of them were motivated by patriotism is impossible to estimate, but it is certain that many put up their names solely to exempt themselves from the unpopular Militia ballot. To ensure that the limited funds allocated to the Volunteer force were well spent, the government instituted a regular system of inspection for the units in every military district. The Inspecting Field Officers, were, as will be seen, zealous in their duty, each corps being inspected upwards of four times in every year. Additionally, Volunteer corps were

44

expected to carry out annually, periods of 'Permanent Duty' in garrison, which gave opportunity for periods of more prolonged and concentrated training. In preparation for invasion, every unit within its area of responsibility earmarked wagons and horses which would be commandeered for their use in the event of such emergency, and the General Officer Commanding the Severn Military District informed commanding officers of the routes of march which their units would follow in order to reach selected concentration points should such action be deemed necessary:

> We learn that the Inspecting Field Officer has called for a Return of the number of Waggons properly fitted up and in readiness with the Volunteer Corps under his inspection, to carry them to any place that may be ordered. We have not seen anything of the kind in this County (Glamorgan), but we understand that throughout the English Counties the Farmers Waggons are all prepared and painted with the name of the Corps to which they are appropriated. [10]

Some few weeks earlier the *Cambrian* had published the following warning:

> It is generally believed that the period of Invasion is now not too far distant. We should constantly be prepared to the fullest extent possible, and we have no doubt that Cambria's Loyal Sons will be found amongst the foremost in the hour of danger, not only to meet and repulse the enemy, but to furnish every requisite, assistance of Waggons, etc, to their Brothers in Arms.

It also published a pamphlet which it stated had been obtained from an American businessman trading with France. Intended for circulation amongst French troops who would form the second and third waves of an invasion force, it reflected a remarkable degree of military confidence:

> French Republic - Army of England, the Sea is passed! the boundaries of nature have yielded to the genius and fortune of the Hero, the Saviour of France: and haughty England already groans under the yoke of her conquerors. London is before you! that Peru of the old world is your prey. Within twenty days I plant the Tricolour Flag on the once proud walls of her execrable Tower! March! the road to Victory is open. [11]

In September 1804 the Glamorgan Volunteer forces were included in Brigadier General Laybourne's Brigade which had it's headquarters at Abergavenny. Their concentration point in the event of invasion was Caerphilly from which town the brigade would march to wherever it was required in South Wales. If, as was more likely, the threat was directed at the south coast of England, the brigade had orders to march via Newport, Monmouthshire and Gloucester to Burford, and there await further orders.[12] Due to the failure of the French fleet to gain control of the English Channel, the Volunteers were never put to the test. Napoleon abandoned the plan and, by August 1805, the great encampments along the French Channel coast had emptied, and the troops which had occupied them directed to pursue his military ambitions elsewhere. The fear of any renewed attempt was finally removed by the British victory at Trafalgar in October – an event which was also to affect the future of the Volunteer movement, as in one decisive stroke the Royal Navy had removed the main reason for its existence. War Secretary Windham in 1806 was very much aware that the terms under which members of Volunteer regiments served, made it virtually impossible for the nation to maintain at full strength its militia and regular army; yet in spite of that fact, he did not so much object to the existence of a Volunteer force, but more to certain classes of men then serving in it:

> My wish is that the Volunteer Corps should consist of such men as it would not be proper to mix with Soldiers of the Line, and whom one would not wish to see serving in the conditions of the common soldier.

Later during the same statement he made it quite clear which section of the population were in his opinion best suited to fight and, if necessary, die.

> The Peasantry - that description of man from whom the Regular Army ought to be recruited should not be shut up in these Volunteer Corps. [13]

The historian Fortescue is also critical, and quite rightly states that the Volunteer force was by that date full of men whose prime motive in serving was avoidance of the Militia Ballot. He also states that many of those more recently joined were described as "Individuals of the most undesirable character".

One can not argue against the truth of Fortescue's first statement but, when all was said and done, the Volunteers did not dictate the terms of service – they simply took advantage of them. As to his second statement, it is a description which fails to fit any Glamorgan Volunteer unit of the period unless one concludes that the constant good reports of both General Officers and Inspecting Field Officers are unreliable. If on the other hand one accepts them to be a true assessment, it becomes clear that some of the best manpower in the county was tied up in the Volunteer force. The year saw a marked slowing down of Volunteer activity with Field Officers Inspections reduced to one per corps per annum and cessation of Permanent Duty. The June Allowances of 1803 were discontinued, and the number of days for which Volunteers could draw pay whilst training were considerably reduced.

A change of government in April 1807 saw Lord Castlereagh succeed Mr Windham as War Secretary, and bring with him some new ideas which were in due course directed to the problem. The government, whilst anxious to retrench, was loth to disband the Volunteer force whilst hostilities continued. Instead, it turned its mind towards reorganisation, and a means which could give it more control of a very large slice of the national manpower. In Glamorgan the year saw a brief return to Volunteer activities reminiscent of 1803, but it was to be fairly short lived.

46

The Inspection of Volunteer Corps is resumed, and we hope that every effort will be exerted to once more revive the spirit and martial ardour of these gallant Bands who have been recently the subject of so much irony and sarcasm. [14]

Some falling off of attendance was inevitable which caused the *Cambrian* to sharply remind the slackers of their obligation:

It appears not to be generally known that all Volunteers are liable to be balloted for the Militia, although they are exempt from service as long as they continue to be effective Volunteers. [15]

Lord Castlreagh's plan for reorganising the force materialised in the form of the Local Militia Act of 1807[16], which allowed for the formation of a new Home Defence Force called the Local Militia and over which the government intended to exercise a much firmer control. In preparation for the change, enrolment in Volunteer units other than Yeomanry was discouraged, and men serving as Infantry Volunteers were actively encouraged to transfer their services into the new force. The response in Glamorgan was heartening, the *Cambrian* announcing on June 3rd:

The exchange of service from the Volunteers to Local Militia is becoming very general. The East Glamorgan Regiment commanded by Colonel Price and Colonel Lascelles's Corps of Riflemen are we understand amongst the number who have agreed to exchange. [17]

The quota of Local Militiamen required from the county was 2,418 private men, which numbers were to be formed into regiments of not less than 700, and not more than 1200 men. The county was to be subdivided into suitable divisions for the maintenance of each regiment, and the Volunteers transferring their services would receive pay as Local Militiamen as from 24 September [18]. At midnight 23 September 1808, the change took place. No ballot was necessary to complete the numbers required, sufficient Volunteers having agreed to serve on in the new force.

Nationally, the Local Militia Act resulted in the creation of 250 regiments of which 27 were Welsh. In some counties some regiments of infantry Volunteers continued to serve on for a period at their own expense, but none as far as is known in Glamorgan. There, only the Yeomanry Cavalry remainded. The infantry volunteers had served their purpose, and almost half a century would pass before their like were to be active again in the county.

NOTES

1. Act 42 Geo 11, c. 66 (Gt Britain)
2. Grenadier and Light Companies
3. Berry, R P *History of the Volunteer Infantry*, pp 81-2
4. South Wales was included in the Severn Military District

5. Act 43 Geo 11, c. 82
6. Act 43 Geo 11, c. 96
7. Berry, R P *History of the Volunteer Infantry.*
8. Fortescue, J W *The County Lieutenancies and the Army, 1803-14.*
9. *Cambrian* 10 February 1804
10. *Cambrian* 27 April 1804
11. *Cambrian,* April 1804
12. *Cambrian,* 7 September 1804
13. Cousins, G *The Defenders.* Muller, 1968
14. *Cambrian* 10 July 1807
15. *Cambrian* 27 November 1807
16. Act 48 Geo 111, c. 111
17. *Cambrian* 3 June 1808
18. *Cambrian* 23 September 1808

Chapter 7
GLAMORGAN VOLUNTEER CORPS, 1803-08

The Swansea Legion, 1803-04

The Swansea Legion was already in the process of reforming when war was declared on 16 May 1803. It had as its mounted arm the Swansea Yeomanry Cavalry which by that date numbered two troops. It's infantry consisted of three companies, drawn as during the previous war, from Swansea and district. The Legion agreed to serve under terms which allowed pay for up to 85 days training per annum.[1] In return, its members agreed to serve when required in any part of the Severn Military District.[2] Before the year was out, they gave further proof of their patriotism by volunteering to extend their services to any part of Great Britain.[3]

The officers gazetted 19 August 1803 were:

Lt Colonel Commandant Thomas Morgan

Cavalry:- Captain Edward Hughes
Captain William Vaughan
Captain John Mills
Cornet David Williams
Cornet Nelson Thomas

Infantry:- Major Roger Landeg (2nd-in-Command)
Captain William Augustus Pengree
Captain Robert Richard Roberts

Lt Henry Pengree
Lt David Bevan
Lt John Morgan
Ensign Phillip Bevan
Ensign Griffith Griffith
Ensign John Habakuk
Surgeon John Davies [4]

In March 1804 the Legion took delivery of two 4lb cannon mounted on field carriages which the officers of the corps had purchased by subscription.[5] The guns were attached to Captain Roberts' company, and a number of men were trained in their use. Presumably some local gunnery expertise was available from members of the Swansea Volunteer Artillery of the previous war. During the same month the Legion was inspected by Colonel Warde [6] who complimented the whole on their high state of discipline and efficiency [7]. In April 1804, a force consisting of the Swansea Legion, West Glamorgan Infantry Volunteers and Lascelles' Glamorgan Riflemen assembled in Swansea to take part in an anti-invasion exercise. The enemy was a force commanded by Captain New, RN, and consisted of a small detachment of soldiers and the crews of the ships of HM Impress Service [8] lying in the port. At the appointed time, and under cover of a cannonade of blank shots, boats, fully manned from the cutter *British Fair*, the tender *Cleveland* and the brigs *Morriston* and *Endeavour* approached the shore. Drawn up on the waterfront to oppose them were the infantry volunteers flanked by field pieces and the cavalry of the Swansea Legion. The defending force, according to one eye witness,

> . . . kept up such a spirited and well directed fire on the enemy that they were speedily driven out of the Harbour. The spirit, steadiness and celerity displayed by the Volunteers entitle them to the highest panegyric, and we have the firmest reliance that in the event of the murderous Consul's bloodstained Legions approaching Cambria's shores her gallant Son's will not be found wanting. [9]

On Monday, 14 May 1804, the infantry companies of the Legion marched to Carmarthen to commence a period of 21 days Permanent Duty.[10] Such periods, similar in many ways to the present day annual camps attended by the Territorial Army, allowed for more concentrated training, and accustomed the volunteers to the duties of troops in garrison. The conduct of the men during the stay in Carmarthen was excellent and earned for the corps the following rather flowery press report :

> The strict attention manifested by the Corps during its stay there to fulfil the laudable purpose for which they had assembled, and their very orderly and soldierlike conduct entitle them to the highest commendation. [11]

The death of Lt Colonel Commandant Morgan towards the end of March heralded the demise of the Swansea Legion. On returning to Swansea from Permanent Duty, its members sought and gained the approval of the authorities to reorganise: the cavalry troops to separate and continue in service independently under the title of Swansea Yeomanry Cavalry, and the infantry companies to reorganise to form a new regiment under the command of William Vaughan (late of the Swansea Cavalry) under the title 'Prince of Wales's Fuzileers'.

> We learn that the late Swansea Legion Infantry have been accepted by His Majesty, by the name of the Glamorgan, or the Prince of Wales's Fuzileers, and the command given to W. Vaughan, Esq, of this town. [12]

This information, which was not available to me when writing the book *Glamorgan, Its Gentlemen and Yeomanry* allows me to correct in this volume the statement then made in good faith regarding the lineage of the Swansea Legion. No information is given in James Willson's chart on the uniform dress of the Swansea Legion Infantry, but it was likely to have been similar to that worn by the regular Light Infantry of the day. An invoice dated 1799, addressed to Lt Colonel Morgan by William Drury, lists amongst other items six cross belt plates for sergeants engraved 'S G L C L' which letters possibly indicate 'Swansea, Gowerland, Llangyfelach, Cilvey Legion and were perhaps brought back into use by the revived Legion in May 1803.

The Cardiff Troop of Yeomanry Cavalry, 1803-08

The renewal of hostilities in May 1803 found the Cardiff Troop fully ready for any service due to the fact that it had not stood down during the short lived peace. A report dated 19 October states:

> The Cardiff Cavalry are daily in expectation of a route to the Gower near Swansea for the protection of that part of the coast. [13]

Such duty was commonplace, and involved coastwatching, beacon duty and assisting the Revenue with anti-smuggling patrols. On 7 October 1804, the Troop was inspected by Colonel Sladden, Inspecting Field Officer for the district, and with good results. [14] On 7 December the unit commenced fourteen days permanent duty in Swansea [15] and on 12 February 1805, was once again put through its paces before Colonel Sladden. In mid May, the Troop met and escorted into Cardiff the Prince of Wales's Fuzileers (Swansea) when they marched to the town for a period of permanent duty [16], and on 19th were involved with them and Lascelles' Glamorgan Riflemen in a grand field day held in the grounds of Sir Robert Blosse's residence at Gabalfa.[17] The Troop having agreed to serve under the June Allowance terms, were allowed pay for up to 85 days training in a year. Full use was made of the training allowance, and the Troop undertook to serve if required in any part of the Severn Military District.

No permanent duty was carried out in 1806 and the round of inspections was much reduced.

On 5 September 1807, the Troop keep the ground on the Castle Green, Cardiff, when a stand of colours was presented to the East Glamorgan Infantry Volunteers. Inspections and permanent duty recommenced during the year, and in early November the Troop marched to Monmouth for a 14 day period of training, where it exercised with the Monmouthshire troops of Yeomanry Cavalry and local regiments of infantry volunteers.

> The strict attention to military duty paid by every member of the Corps during their short period of service justly entitle them to the commendation they received from their worthy Captain, as well as from the hospitable inhabitants of Monmouth who expressed much regret at their quitting the town. [18]

The venue for its 1808 Permanent Duty was Cardiff which training commenced on 21 May. During that period the Troop exercised with the Usk infantry volunteers from Monmouthshire who were also in Cardiff for similar training. [19]

Troop Standard: On Monday 20 June, the Troop was inspected by Colonel Madden and received his compliments on their efficiency and discipline.[20] It was unaffected by the changes brought about in the Volunteer Force due to the implimentation of the Local Militia Act and it's story will be continued in a later chapter.

On Wednesday 21 June 1804, the Cardiff Troop was presented with a guidon by Mrs Wyndham, wife of Thomas Wyndham, MP, Vice Lieutenant of the county. The presentation, at which Mrs Wyndham deputised for the donor, the Marchioness of Bute, took place in the grounds of Cardiff Castle and was attended by most of the gentry of Glamorgan and the neighbouring counties, most of whom were present in town for the first day of the Glamorgan Races. The guidon was consecrated by the Reverend Davies of Wenvoe, after which Mrs Wyndham presented it to Captain Wood and addressed him in the following words:

> Captain Wood, In the name of my highly esteemed friend, the Marchioness of Bute, I present you with this Standard as a token of the respect she bears for the Corps commanded by you. To myself, it affords considerable pleasure when I reflect on the honour to deliver it to the protection of those, who truly animated with the spirit of Ancient Britons, will, I am convinced, preserve it to their last extremity. [20]
> Captain Woods's reply was in perfect unison with the above, and in the name of the Corps, expressed a deep and grateful sense that they should ever entertain the honour done them by the Marchioness, and of the very handsome manner in which it was conveyed, and that he was fully convinced, that there was not an individual in the

Troop but would preserve it with his very existence. The ground was kept by the Cardiff Volunteer Infantry. The Officers of the Corps, together with several Gentlemen of respectability afterwards dined with the Troop in the Cardiff Arms. [21]

The guidon has fortunately survived, and is today preserved in the Welsh Folk Museum at St Fagan. A swallow tailed flag of gold damask with gold fringe, it carries at the centre, within the Union a wreath and the corps title in gold letters. At the top left and bottom right hand corners is displayed the white horse of Hanover within a gold enclosure. In the other two corners, a rose and thistle motif, similarly enclosed. The reverse of the guidon carries a similar design, and it has scarlet and gold tassels.

Uniform Dress and Accoutrements: The head-dress consisted of a Tarleton helmet (a helmet of the light dragoon pattern), with black fur crest and silver fittings. On its left side was displayed a large white feather plume, and the base of the headpiece was decorated with a band of leopard skin, wound turban fashion, and secured by silver chains. A silver plated band above the peak carried the unit's title.

A short scarlet jacket had tails embellished with silver braid, and had cuffs and

Guidon, Cardiff Troop of Yeomanry Cavalry.
[National Museum of Wales (Welsh Folk Museum)]

collar faced with yellow cloth edged with silver braid. The chest was decorated with bars of silver cord and three rows of silver buttons. The collar was cut away to reveal the black neck stock and a portion of white shirt frill. A crimson sash was worn around the waist, knotted, with tassels hanging at the right front. White doeskin breeches worn with silver trimmed black hessian boots and spurs completed the outfit.

The uniform described was that worn by officers. That worn by other ranks was similar but less decorative. White metal and white cord substituting for silver and silver braid.

The sword belt was worn under the sash by officers with two white patent leather slings supporting a stirrup hilted light cavalry sabre in a polished steel scabbard. Over the left shoulder was worn a white leather belt supporting a black patent leather ammunition pouch (or cartouche) on the back. Other ranks sword belts and shoulder belts were made of white buff leather and the ammunition pouch of black leather. Pistol holsters, harness and saddle were of plain brown leather, the former covered with black lambswool flounces. A black saddle cloth was worn, and a brown leather valise was strapped on the back of the saddle to carry the cape. Sabres and pistols and 12 carbines were supplied to the Troop by Ordnance.

The Fairwood Troop of Yeomanry Cavalry, 1803-08

The Fairwood Troop, not having disbanded in April 1802, was fully ready for service when war was declared in May 1803. Still commanded by Sir Gabriel Powell, the Troop on 12 October 1804, joined Lt Colonel Llewelyn's West Glamorgan Volunteer Infantry for exercises on the Crumlin Burrows, where both units were inspected by Colonel Sladden, District Inspector of Volunteers.

> The Inspection has shown that the Corps has lost not a particle of their former distinguished reputation, and the Colonel was pleased to express his unqualified approbation of the whole. [22]

On the 27 May 1805, the Troop marched to Cowbridge to commence 14 days of Permanent Duty. During their stay in the town, they exercised with the local volunteers and their good conduct and professionalism brought them much credit both on and off duty.[23] On June 14th, the Troop paraded in Swansea with the Prince of Wales's Infantry Volunteers and were inspected by Colonel Sladden, again with good results.[24] No Permanent Duty was carried out in 1806. The establishment of the Troop in that year was: 1 captain commandant, 2 subalterns, 1 staff officer, 2 sergeants, 2 corporals, 1 trumpeter and 60 private men but, strangely, despite the previous good inspection reports only 38 of the yeomen were returned as 'efficient'.

In June 1807, the Troop joined with the Swansea Cavalry and Prince of Wales's Fuzileers for a Grand Review on the Swansea Burrows to celebrate the King's birthday.

The Ships in Harbour displayed their Colours and Streamers. The *Morriston* Armed Brig and the *Eliza* Tender fired a Royal Salute. The Prince of Wales's Fuzileers and the Fairwood and the Swansea Cavalry assembled on the Burrows where several volleys were fired.[25]

The Troop was inspected by Colonel Madden in August and again in October. One therefore presumes that by those dates a greater number of men were being returned as 'efficient'. They commenced a period of 14 days permanent duty in Swansea on 10 November [26], and in 1808 assembled twice in the same town for that purpose, once in September and again in November.

The Troop remained in service after 1808 which story continues in another chapter.

No record has been found which refers to a presentation of a standard to this unit. Its dress and accoutrements were similar to those worn by the Cardiff Troop.[27]

The Glamorgan Riflemen, 1803-08

Raised from the town and rural district surrounding Cardiff by Rowley Lascelles, the Riflemen were accepted for service on 12 July 1803. Their role was based on that of the regular rifle units, whose style and shade of dress (rifle green) and drill movements it copied.

The establishment of this regiment was set at: 2 field officers, 4 captains, 12 lieutenants and 2nd lieutenants, 19 sergeants, 24 corporals, 6 drummers/ buglers and 390 private men divided into 6 companies of 65 volunteers each.

The unit served under terms associated with the June Allowances, and were therefore allowed pay for up to 85 days training in any one year. In return, it was expected to be on call to serve if required in any part of the Severn Military District, but as an expression of its patriotism, went further, by volunteering to serve in any part of Great Britain in the event of national emergency.

On 3 April 1804, the corps marched to Swansea to commence a period of Permanent Duty.[28] During that three week period it had the opportunity to exercise with the volunteers of Swansea and district and also accustom both officers and men to duties in garrison. In company with the Swansea Legion and West Glamorgan Infantry it took part in an anti-invasion exercise, and at St Nicholas on the 19 May was inspected by Colonel Warde, Inspecting Field Officer. The Colonel expressed great satisfaction with their progress and appearance.[29]

Together with other Glamorgan units, the Riflemen were in September 1804 included in Brigadier Laybourne's Brigade with Caerphilly nominated as assembly point in the event of invasion, from whence the Brigade would march to Burford, Oxfordshire to await further orders.[30]

The Government were not over-generous to volunteer corps in terms of financial assistance, and in consequence the maintenance of weapons and a reasonable standard of uniform clothing was for many units an ever present problem. The more zealous the corps, the quicker did its clothing wear out, and such was the case with the Glamorgan Riflemen. In a letter to the Secretary of State dated 9 July [31] Lt Colonel Lascelles complained that "Eighty five days drill and twenty one days of permanent duty have reduced the Clothing allowed to my Corps by Government to rags". How the Colonel resolved the problem is not known, but very likely by tapping his own pocket and those of his officers and friends. During the year 1805 the Riflemen were inspected on five occasions, each time with good results, and on 19 May joined the Prince of Wales's Fuzileers of Swansea for manoeuvres which were held in the grounds of Sir Robert Blosse's residence at Gabalfa, Cardiff.[32]

The venue for the Riflemen's own period of Permanent Duty is not known, but was very likely to have been Newport or Swansea. Such activities were discontinued for the year 1806, but in 1807 they marched to Abergavenny, Monmouthshire returning to Cardiff on 26 October on completion of an eleven day stint.

> The Glamorgan Riflemen commanded by that able Officer, Colonel Lascelles marched into Cardiff on their return from Abergavenny having performed eleven days of permanent duty with great credit to themselves, and the satisfaction of their Commanding Officer. During their stay at Abergavenny, they each day marched to the grounds of the residence of Hanbury Williams, Esq, near Colebrook, which the owner indulged them with the use of for the purposes of their Field Exercises. There they fired in Battalion, and in Companies, in extended order, kneeling, and on the ground. The situation was particularly adapted to the performance of the various evolutions, and the Rifle exercises, which they went through with great precision and correctness. [33]

Whilst on Permanent Duty the Riflemen were billeted on the inns and common lodging houses of the town in the same manner as regular troops. To their credit, their behaviour in those circumstances was such as to set an example which certain regiments of the line would have done well to emulate.

In September 1808, the Glamorgan Riflemen stood down as a volunteer body, but the majority of its officers and men continued in service without break due to having enrolled themselves in the newly formed regiment of East Glamorgan Local Militia.[34]

The Fforest Riflemen, 1803-08

Raised by Major Thomas Lockwood from the Fforest district near Swansea, the Fforest Riflemen were accepted for service on 19 August 1803. The term 'Riflemen' suggests that, like Rowley Lascelles' Glamorgan Riflemen, the unit adopted rifle green dress, black leather accoutrements and a style of drill and field movement peculiar to the regular Rifle Corps. This cannot be confirmed as its dress is not listed in James Willson's *Volunteer Chart*. The establishment of this corps was set at 1 field officer, 3 captains, 3 lieutenants, 3 second lieutenants, 9 sergeants, 9 corporals, 3 drummers/buglers and 201 private men divided amongst three companies.

On 5 February 1804, the corps was inspected by Colonel Warde, District Inspecting Field Officer, with good results, and again on 11 October by Colonel Sladden.[35] A third inspection took place on 2 December, but no record has been found of the unit completing a period of Permanent Duty in that year. The report of an inspection which took place in February 1805, refers to the corps as Major Lockwood's Rangers[36], and likewise when reporting Brigadier General Bowton's visit on 14 April.

> Sunday last, Brigadier General Bowton inspected Major Lockwood's Rangers at Fforest and expressed himself particularly gratified with their manoeuvres, as being peculiarly adapted to the nature of the country they would have to defend in the event of Invasion. [37]

On 4 June 1805, the Riflemen joined other local volunteer units at the King's birthday parade in Swansea at which a *feu de joie* was fired and, on being inspected by Colonel Sladden in October, "they received well merited compliments on their appearance and discipline". [38]

On 4 June 1807, the corps was again present in Swansea for the King's birthday celebrations, and on 4 August paraded at Fforest for inspection by Colonel Madden.

> On Tuesday, Colonel Madden inspected the Fforest Rifle Corps commanded by Captain Jeffries in the absence of Major Lockwood, with whose manoeuvres and advanced state of discipline he expressed himself particularly gratified.[39]

The Riflemen were still meriting praise from the Inspecting Field Officers in June 1808, which is the last time that mention of their activities is made in the *Cambrian*. No mention is ever made of them being out on Permanent Duty between 1804 and 1808, and that is very likely due to the possibility that their terms of service did not extend to duties outside their own locality. If that was the case, then their running costs must have been almost wholly covered by Major Lockwood himself, or by subscription made locally, or perhaps by a combination of both.

In September 1808, the Fforest Riflemen stood down, but a number of their officers and men, including Thomas Lockwood himself (who appears as a Major in the Local Militia List of 1810), transferred their services into the West Glamorgan Regiment of Local Militia.

The Eastern Glamorgan Infantry Volunteers, 1803-08

Raised in 1803 by John Price of Llandaff Court, this unit was also on occasion referred to both as the 2nd Glamorgan Regiment of Volunteers and as the East Glamorgan Infantry. Accepted for service on 5 October 1803, its establishment was set at 3 field officers, 12 captains, 24 lieutenants and second lieutenants, 36 sergeants, 36 corporals, 12 drummers and 822 private men divided into 9 companies each numbering 67 volunteers and 3 companies each numbering 73 volunteers, which were raised across the administrative division now known as Mid Glamorgan.

Officers serving as at 16 November 1803, were:

Lt Colonel John Price of Llandaff Court
Major John Bassett of Bonviston House
Captain William Meyrick of Merthyr Tydfil
Captain Robert Jones
Captain Thomas Thomas,
Captain Watkin George of Merthyr Tydfil
Captain J Bruce Knight
Captain Wyndham Lewis of Cardiff
Captain Gann Wilkins of Merthyr Tydfil
Captain Evan Samuels [40]

On 19 March 1804, the Pentyrch and Caerphilly Companies, being respectively No 1 and No 4 Companies of the corps assembled in a field near the Nantgarw Turnpike where they were inspected by Colonel Warde. The Colonel was pleased to express his approbation of their military appearance and discipline and general state of efficiency.[41]

On 16 April the Colonel inspected the three Merthyr companies with similar satisfactory results, the Volunteers "to a man consented to go on permanent duty for 21 days".[42] During the same month the Colonel called for a Return to be submitted of the number of waggons properly fitted out as transport which together with horses would be commandeered in the event of emergency. [43] No record of the numbers returned has been found, but there can be no doubt that the Colonel received the results he required.

On 25 May, the Eastern Corps marching in two divisions converged on Swansea where it was to be in garrison for 21 days Permanent Duty. The period proved to be highly instructive for the 800 of all ranks who were present [44] and at an inspection on June 7th,

Gorget, East Glamorgan Infantry Volunteers, c1803.
[Wallis & Wallis]

> . . . Colonel Warde, who after seeing them go through their different manoeuvres was pleased to express himself perfectly satisfied with their military appearance and progress in discipline. [45]

The return to Merthyr Tydfil of the three local companies of the Eastern Glamorgan Infantry created great excitement and merited press coverage of the sort usually reserved for veterans returning from some great military victory, as opposed to the return to the town of a group of part-time soldiers who had spent a quite pleasant and none too strenuous three week break in Swansea.

> They were met by a vast concourse of their fellow townspeople, and the joy that pervaded all ranks at the safe return of those who had volunteered their lives and fortune in defence of the Country is not to be expressed. Immediately after their arrival in town, they were formed in a circle and addressed by Captain Meyrick in an elegant and majestic speech, thanking them for their exemplary conduct whilst on duty. [46]

This reaction by the the townsfolk of Merthyr can be attributed to the fact that a member of the Merthyr Tydfil company, a man named John Griffiths, had lost his life during the Swansea training when, during an exercise, he had somehow contrived to be standing in front of the muzzle of one of the Swansea Legion's cannon at the moment of firing. By so doing, he earned himself the dubious honour of being, as far as is known, of being the only Glamorgan Volunteer to die on what might be termed as 'home based wartime service'. The anticlimax came with the announcement that £11 had been raised for relief of his widow and family.[47]

In October, Colonel Sladden commenced his inspection with the companies of the Cardiff Division on the 7th and those of Merthyr on the 15th [48] His opinion was summed up in the statement that the volunteers "were inferior to none in the Kingdom" which comment prompted the delighted officers to treat the men to an excellent dinner on completion of the inspection. Colonel Sladden's next visit to took place in February 1805, when once again he expressed himself "much gratified with their appearance and discipline." [49]

On 11 May 1805, the Eastern Corps again assembled in Swansea for a 21 period of Permanent Duty. The month saw Major Price promoted Lieutenant Colonel and Captain Bassett to Major to fill the vacancy. Colonel Price was also delighted to receive a letter from the Marquis of Bute signifying his intention of presenting the unit with a stand of colours.[50] No Permanent Duty was entered into in 1806, but training continued on an individual company basis. On 29 October 1807, the whole assembled in Cardiff for ten days Permanent Duty, and on 5 November paraded on the Cardiff Castle green to receive from the Marquis of Bute the stand of colours promised to them more than two years previously.

> The Regiment was drawn up on the Castle Green, the ground being kept by the Cardiff Cavalry, when the Reverend Benjamin Hall, DD, consecrated the Colours in a most impressive manner. Afterwards, Colonel Price addressed the Corps in a neat and appropriate speech, and it can be truly said that Cardiff has seldom witnessed a scene so interesting and animating. In the evening the Officers of the Corps entertained a large party of friends at Dinner in the Cardiff Arms. In order that each member of the Regiment might partake of the festivities of the day, seven barrels of Stout were distributed amongst the Non Commissioned Officers and Privates. [51]

In 1808, Cardiff again provided the facilities for the Permanent Duty, with the corps assembling for 14 days commencing on 7 May. This was to be the Eastern Regiment's last assembly as a volunteer unit as in September 1808 it stood down, and the majority of its officers and men transferred their services to the newly formed regiment of East Glamorgan Local Militia.

The uniform worn by the Eastern Glamorgan Infantry Volunteers was similar to that worn by John Llewelyn's Western Regiment, namely a red coat with yellow facings. No trace of the colours or record of their disposal has been found, but it is likely, that in accordance with accepted custom they were handed back to the donor for safe-keeping shortly after the stand down, or alternatively remained in possession of the Commanding Officer.

The Western Glamorgan Infantry Volunteers, 1803-08

Raised in 1803 by John Llewelyn of Penllergaer, near Swansea, West Glamorgan, this force, which was accepted for service on 5 October, was for the greater part a resurrection of the old Glamorgan Rangers Volunteers which had stood down in April 1802. The unit, also often referred to as both the West Glamorgan Infantry and the Western Regiment, had a large catchment extending from the Gower in the west, through Swansea and Neath to Bridgend in the east. In consequence, except when on Permanent Duty it trained and exercised by companies and in groups known as the Western, Central and Eastern Divisions. Its establishment was fixed at 3 field officers, 11 captains, 22 lieutenants and 2nd lieutenants, 33 sergeants, 33 corporals, 11 drummers, and 737 private men divided amongst eleven companies.

Officers serving in November 1803 were:

> Lt Colonel John Llewelyn of Penllergaer
> Lt Colonel Thomas Wyndham of Dunraven
> Major Richard Hoare Jenkins
> Captain John Hancorne
> Captain John Nathaniel Myers
> Captain John Morris
> Captain George Wynch
> Captain John May
> Captain James Coke
> Captain George Haynes
> Captain Robert Sydney
> Captain Thomas Hobbes
> Captain Reynold Thomas Deare [52]

On 30 March 1804, the seven companies of the Western and Central Divisions assembled in Swansea, and later marched to Crumlin Burrows where they were inspected by the District Inspector, Colonel Warde. The Eastern Division Companies had been inspected at Bridgend on 25 March, and the Colonel expressed satisfaction with their overall progress and efficiency.[53]

Monday 16 April was a fine spring day, and drew out spectators in their hundreds to witness the Volunteers engaged in an anti-invasion exercise. Assembling on the shore, near the harbour, the Volunteers together with the Swansea Legion and Lascelles's Glamorgan Riflemen, all under the command of Lt Colonel Llewelyn, were seen to repulse successfully an enemy represented by a small detachment of soldiers and the crews of Naval Impressment Service vessels stationed in the port.

On Sunday 20 May 1805, four companies of the Eastern Division were inspected by Colonel Warde at Corntown, near Bridgend and on the next day, the Central and Western Divisions Companies at Fforest, Swansea. Sadly, inclement weather did much to hamper the proceedings, "The Inspecting Field Officer, after having seen the Troops go through part of their exercises, very much to their credit, declined to keep the Corps longer under Arms in very heavy rain. " [54]

On 5 June, the eleven companies assembled in Swansea prior to marching to Carmarthen to commence a four-teen day period of permanent duty. There they were brigaded with the 2nd Regiment of Carmarthenshire Volunteers assembled in the town for the same purpose.[55]

In December, the Western Glamorgan Infantry Volunteers received their fourth inspection for that year, when Colonel Sladden, Inspecting Field Officer commencing on the 5th of the month, inspected the six Swansea and Neath companies on the 5th and the remaining four companies at Bridgend on the following day. The Colonel expressed great satisfaction with the zeal and discipline displayed by the corps.[56]

On 12 February 1805, there commenced another round of inspection with Colonel Sladden visiting first the Western Division at Swansea and moving on during the week to inspect the other divisions at Neath and Bridgend. The *Cambrian,* reporting the results on 15 February, stated that "their ardour appeared unabated, their discipline improved, they gave the Inspecting Officer complete satis-faction".

Between 17 and 19 April. the three Divisions in turn exercised for the benefit of Brigadier General Bowton, who like the Inspecting Field Officers was suitably impressed. On 3 June they assembled in Swansea for 15 days permanent duty and on the following day celebrated the King's birthday at a Grand Field Day in company with other volunteer units – an event which drew out many spectators from the town and surrounding district.

Cross belt plate, Western Regiment of Glamorgan Infantry Volunteers, 1803-8. [Welch Regiment Museum]

The Line was formed at about 12 o'clock on the beach confronting the sea, and comprised of the Pembroke Cavalry [57] commanded by Major Colby on the right, the Swansea Cavalry, Captain Hughes on the left, the Prince of Wales's Fuzileers, Colonel Vaughan, the Fforest Rangers, Captain Jeffries, and the Western Glamorgan Regiment, Colonel Llewelyn, composed the centre. [58]

The parade was commanded by Lt Colonel Llewelyn, and the troops later fired a *feu de joie* before continuing with a demonstration of field exercises and drill manouevres.

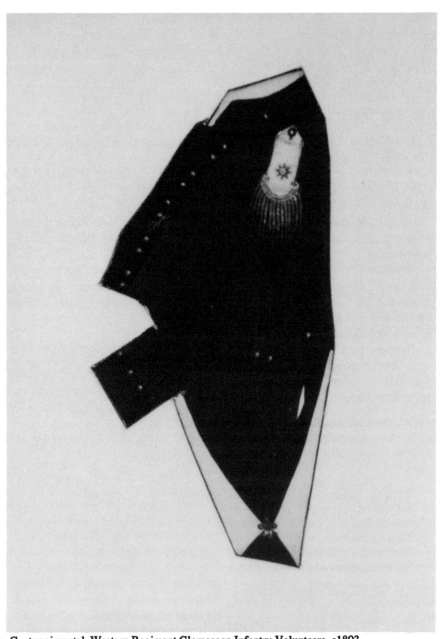

Coat regimental, Western Regiment Glamorgan Infantry Volunteers, c1803.

On the 14th of the month the corps paraded to receive a stand of colours from the hands of Mrs Llewelyn, their Colonel's lady. The colours were a gift from the Marquis of Bute. The unit was formed into hollow square on the Burrows, into which formation, Mrs Llewelyn, accompanied by two sergeants carrying the colours entered at the appointed hour. After a service of consecration, conducted by the Reverend Bassett, Mrs Llewelyn presented the colours to the Commanding Officer with the following words:

At the request of the Marchioness of Bute, I have the honour to present you with the Colours given by the Lord Lieutenant to your Corps. I have singular pleasure in committing them to your associates in arms, persuaded that they are entrusted to Men worthy of the sacred charge. History furnishes many brilliant examples of Cambrian valour, and I am impressed with the fullest confidence, that should such exertions be called for to repel an immediate enemy, every individual in this Corps will be ready to defend his King, his Country and his Colours with a zeal as loyal, and a courage as undaunted as ever shone conspicuous in the actions of their bravest ancestors.

to which Lt Colonel Llewelyn replied,

The honour done the regiment by the Marchionesss of Bute in presenting, and the flattering mark of esteem of our Lord Lieutenant in giving and confiding these Colours to our charge demand our warmest acknowledgement. By this token of regard, a confidence is placed in the Corps which I hope they will fully merit, and I trust the Standards are committed to Men willing to defend and determined to protect them unsullied by dishonourable stain. It would ill become me to become panegyrist on my own Countrymen, yet I may venture to assert that the Welsh have been justly esteemed as a valourous people. If the day of trial should arrive, I will not doubt the exertions of this Corps in defence of their Country. Expressed in their own language, they would feel it were better to suffer death than shame.

After the Colonel had concluded, he turned to the men and called out aloud the Welsh Motto - 'Gwell Angau na Chywilydd' which was hailed by three hearty cheers expressive of the gallant fellows concurrence in the patriotic sentiment. The Regiment then fell into Line, and the Colours were paraded in front, and the Ensigns took up their proper stations. The Battalion then advanced a few paces forward and fired three capital volleys. They were then drawn up in Wind Street, where their Motto was again called to their recollection, and again cordially cheered - Gwell Angau na Chywilydd. [59]

The training period ended on a high note, particularly as the conduct of the men both on and off duty had been exemplary.

In August, the corps together with its transport was inspected by Colonel Sladden who "found them all improved in discipline and ready to meet the vaunting foe which has so long threatened us with Invasion. " [60]

Further visits by the Colonel in October and December completed for 1805 the annual round of inspections.

Following an Inspection in April 1806, the House of Commons was informed that the Western Glamorgan Regiment was not only ready for any service, but was fit to act with troops of the Line [61] – a compliment not easily come by, and proof once again that Volunteers, in Glamorgan at least, were not the rag, tag and bobtail country bumkins which were lampooned by certain caricaturists of that period. As previously noted, they were, disregarding the motive which brought them to such service, better quality men in most respects, than any man left to fall prey to the recruiters of the Line.

Volunteer activity was, due to the recent victory at Trafalgar and the removal of French troops from the Channel coast, much less marked in 1806, and no permanent duty training took place. In 1807 the venue for the annual permanent duty was again Swansea, but only for a shorter period of ten days.

On 4 June, the Western Division paraded in Swansea to celebrate the King's birthday:

> The Anniversary of Our Beloved Sovereign's Birthday was celebrated in this Town yesterday with the most ardent loyalty. The Ships in the harbour displayed their Colours and Streamers. The *Morriston* Armed Brig and the Tender *Eliza* fired the Royal Salute, and four Companies of the Western Glamorgan and the Fforest Riflemen exercised in Brigade at Fforest and fired a Feu de Joie. [62]

Wednesday 1 June 1808, saw the Western Glamorgan Corps assembled in Swansea in preparation for its march to Carmarthen and eight days of permanent duty. Prior to departure, Lt Colonel Llewelyn addressed all ranks:

> The Colonel in a neat and appropriate address, reminded the Men of the honour they had obtained when last at Carmarthen, the Corporation of the Town having expressed their public approbation of their soldierlike behaviour by a Vote of Thanks. He exhorted them to preserve their high character by steadily persevering in that line of conduct which had rendered them so worthy of so distinguished a compliment. (63)

During its stay in Carmarthen, the corps was brigaded with the Prince of Wales's Fuzileers, another Swansea unit, present in the town for the same training purpose. Both regiments joined with Carmarthenshire Volunteers in celebrating the King's birthday in true military style on June 4th.

On returning to Swansea, the corps completed what remained of its fourteen day training embodiment in that town, and was dismissed on the 14th. [64]

In September 1808, the Western Glamorgan Infantry Volunteers stood down, but the majority of its officers and men continued in service having voluntarily tranferred to the newly raised Regiment of West Glamorgan Local Militia.

Uniform dress: According to James Willson's Chart, this consisted of a red jacket with yellow facings and white breeches. It is likely that such a large formation had both Grenadier and Light Companies. Both they and the battalion companies would have been dressed in much the same style as their contemporaries serving in the Regiments of the Line.

Marksmanship Medal (obverse & reverse), Neath Company,
Western Glamorgan Infantry Volunteers, 1803.
[J L Balmer, TD]

Colours: The stand of colours which was presented to the Regiment does not appear to have survived, but undoubtedly passed back into the hands of the donor or to John Llewelyn of Penllergaer. It is interesting to note that the use of the Welsh Motto *Gwell Angau na Chywilydd* by this Corps on their Colours preceded the adoption of the same motto by the 41st (The Welch) Regiment of Infantry some 26 years later. It may well be the case, that Lt Colonel Edmund Keynton Williams, Commanding Officer of the 41st Foot in 1831, a native of Monmouthshire, had at one time or another during the Napoleonic Wars seen the colours of the Western Glamorgan Infantry, and as a result, was inspired to adopt the same motto for use by his regiment on its territorialisation in 1831, and so link it quite firmly with Wales.

The Glamorgan (Prince of Wales's Fuzileers) Volunteers, 1804-08

In August 1804, the infantry companies of the disbanding Swansea Legion received permission to continue in service under the title Glamorgan, or Prince of Wales's Fuzileers, under the command of Lt Colonel William Vaughan, one time Captain in the Swansea Cavalry. In consequence, the date of acceptance of this Corps is August 1804, but at the same time one must bear in mind that its

65

members had served with the disbanded Swansea Legion since 12 July, 1803.

The establishment of the regiment included 1 field officer, 3 captains and 400 private men divided amongst 8 companies. By mid-year 1804, the corps was progressing favourably, and after an inspection by Colonel Sladden in October "deservingly obtained very flattering compliments on theirmilitary appearance and high state of discipline. " [65]

In 1805, the round of inspections commenced on 13 February when Colonel Sladden visited. He was followed on 20 April by Brigadier General Bowton, and on both occasions the keeness and ability of the Corps was the subject of favourable comment. On 6 May, the Fuzileers assembled in Swansea and then marched off to Cardiff to commence a four week period of permanent duty.

> The Fuzileers on their march to Cardiff last week were received at Bridgend with a ringing of bells and every possible mark of respect. About a mile from Cardiff they found Captain Wood's Troop of Cavalry drawn up to receive them, which, after saluting the Corps, escorted it into the town, where they were treated with great attention by all ranks. The Men behaved extremely well on the march, and their conduct in Quarters merits the civilities which they experience. [66]

In Cardiff on 19 May, the Corps, brigaded with Lascelles' Glamorgan Riflemen, accepted the use of Sir Robert Blosse's grounds at Gabalfa for combined field exercises and manoeuvres, and in all spent a most instructive few weeks in the town before setting off for Swansea on the 29th.

> On the march home, friends of the Colonel and other inhabitants of Llantrisant provided a plentiful supply of bread and cheese and good Welsh Ale to regale the Soldiers, during which the Officers returned to the Mansion of the Reverend Mr Rickards where a very elegant party of Ladies added grace to the scene. The Regiment then proceeded to Lt Colonel Jenkins's hospitable seat at Llanharan where the Officers were entertained to a military lejune. [67]

The regiment stayed overnight at Bridgend, moving on to Swansea early on the morning of 29 May. Captain Evans's company order book states "Bridgend - The first Drum will beat at 3 o'clock tomorrow morning and the second at half past three and march immediately." The *Cambrian* reporting their progress stated:

> The Column of March and the embarkation and debarkation at the Briton Ferry and Swansea Rivers was accompanied by their excellent Band playing 'God Save The King' and 'Rule Britannia' as the Colours were passing over, and would have done credit to the oldest Regiment.

The next event came on June 4th, when the corps assembled with other local volunteer units to celebrate the King's birthday in military fashion, when Colonel John Llewelyn of Penllergaer took command of the parade. No permanent duty was entered into in 1806, and although inspections continued, they were less frequent. For that which took place in April, the corps was brigaded with the

Western Division of the Western Glamorgan Infantry, Colonel Sladden expressing great satisfaction with their drill and smart appearance.

The venue for permanent duty in 1807 was Swansea and took place in November.[68] On the 4th of that month Captain Evans's Order Book states:

Orders for Parade - Swansea
Arms Flinted with full complement of blank Cartridges.
Great Coats neatly rolled. Knapsacks well filled with Necessaries.

The following officers are mentioned:

> Lt Thomas Jones
> Lt William Jones
> Lt William Gronow
> Lt Caton
> Lt Byne
> Lt MacAdam
> Ensign Gunthorpe
> Ensign Rees
> Ensign Child
> Ensign Michael

The *Cambrian* reporting the completion of that permanent duty stated:

They are a fine body of men, the standard of the Regiment being that of the Guards. The weather was remarkably unfavourable for Field Duty notwithstanding, the exercise of the Corps came on with great alacrity. This Regiment justly prides itself on its appointments and the state of its Arms, being the result of careful inspection of the Arms and Necessaries in which only 1 Greatcoat and 1 Knapsack were found wanting. This sufficiently manifests the attention paid to this side of service. They expended their full allowance of Ammunition and honeycombed the Targets, in which the Band, for their number, put in most holes and showed themselves expert Marksmen. Their individual firing with ball cartridge would not have discredited a Regiment which had seen service. Our worthy Borough Magistrate requested the Lieutenant Colonel to express his thanks for the orderly conduct of the Non Commissioned Officers and Men during their stay in Quarters, and the Lieutenant Colonel addressed the Men previous to lodging the Colours after the completion of duty in both the English and Welsh languages; expressing the Officers and his own approbation of their soldierlike conduct and discipline, and hoping that when they laid aside their Arms they would equally distinguish themselves by their peaceable and correct conduct as private individuals and members of society.

On 15 April 1808, the regiment was inspected by Colonel Madden, Inspecting Field Officer, who congratulated Lt Colonel Vaughan in having so fine a body of men under his command, and also Captain Roberts for his work as Adjutant. Addressing the men, he impressed upon them the absolute necessity for undeviating attention to instructions as only in that way would they remain efficient soldiers.

At this date the five companies were commanded by:

No 1 Captain Mansfield
No 2 Captain Evans
No 3 Captain Bevan
No 4 Captain Jones
No 5 Captain Eaton

Assembling in Swansea on the evening of Sunday 22 May 1808, the Prince of Wales' Fuzileers Volunteers set off early the following morning for Haverfordwest and a period of permanent duty. About three miles outside Carmarthen they were met by the 3rd Bn Carmarthenshire Infantry Volunteers under the command of Major Brown, who escorted them to their parade ground in Carmarthen. That evening Lt Colonel Vaughan and the officers of the Fuzileers dined the officers of the Carmarthenshire Infantry Volunteers in the Ivy Bush Hotel, whilst the Glamorgan men, who had with their band made quite an impression on the townspeople on their arrival, received in the evening their full hospitality. Early the next morning the Fuzileers resumed the march to Haverfordwest [69], a hive of military activity in those days, arriving there on the Wednesday, and increased the garrison to upwards of 1,000 soldiers. It is recorded that the last 32 miles of the march, including halts, was completed in 12 hours, but allowing for a 10 minute halt every hour, their progress by modern standards was in no way spectacular, as a battalion on route march should cover at least 4 miles in every hour.

The regiment was made very welcome in the town and brigaded with the Fishguard Infantry Volunteers who were also on permanent duty in the garrison. During its stay in the Haverfordwest garrison, the Glamorgan unit was inspected by Colonel Stewart, Officer Commanding the Haverfordwest Division, Severn Military District, who expressed his great satisfaction with the performance of both the Glamorgan and Pembrokeshire corps and particularly with their knowledge of field work and skill at live firing.

On 4 June, the Fuzileers then on their way home halted at Carmarthen and there took part in the local King's birthday celebrations [70] before marching on through Kidwelly and Llanelli. At Lougher Ford, they found the river swollen by recent rain and a half tide but, not being inclined to wait for more favourable conditions, they followed the colours and the band by wading waist deep through the water and, after a halt at the home of Mr Pengree whose son was a Captain in the corps, resumed their march for Swansea [71].

On 23 September, the Glamorgan Fuzileers assembled for the last time as a volunteer corps, and on the following day continued in service as companies of the newly formed West Glamorgan Local Militia. During the final parade, Lt Colonel Vaughan thanked the Men for their loyal service and for

> . . . their uniform attention and the steadiness they had manifested while Volunteers, and expressed his conviction that their military ardour would suffer no diminuation by the exchange of service. [72]

It is interesting to note that in 1805, this regiment had volunteered for general service with the Army, an offer most gratefully acknowledged, but not taken advantage of by the Crown. No record has been found of any other Welsh volunteer unit making such a spirited offer, and it may well be that it was the only one in the Principality to do so.

Colours: At a date prior to May 1805 the Prince of Wales' Fuzileers received a stand of colours, but no record of the donor or of the presentation ceremony has been found. The Regimental Colour survives in a very delapidated condition and

Regimental Colour, Glamorgan or Prince of Wales's Fuzileer
Volunteers, 1804-8.
[National Museum of Wales: Welsh Folk Museum]

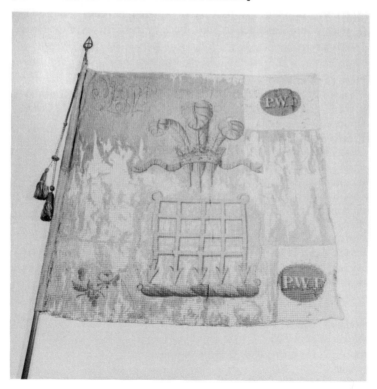

is at present preserved in the Welsh Folk Museum at St Fagan. The backcloth is a faded blue which was at one time a royal blue. Other details can be seen in the accompanying photograph.

Uniform: They wore a red jacket with blue facings and white breeches. The title 'Fuzileers' and such records as have been found relating to this corps suggests that they were dressed in a uniform patterned on that worn by the 23rd Foot (The Royal Welch Fusiliers) of the day, and that Vaughan and his officers dug deeply into their own pockets to maintain a smart turn out at all times.

The Cardiff Volunteer Artillery

Although no official or press record has been found which gives details of the raising and activities of an artillery corps of this name, there exists a Medal of Merit inscribed 'Cardiff Volunteer Artillery' presented in 1804 to Thomas Jones by the 'Officers of the Battery'. The present location of this medal is unknown but it is described as being of engraved silver with a raised rim and having a diameter of 60mm. The obverse depicts a trophy of cannon and associated material and carries the corps title and the inscription 'Reward of Merit, 1804'. The reverse bears the inscription 'Presented to Thos Jones by the Officers of the Battery' [73].

NOTES

1. The June Allowances
2. The District covered the whole of South Wales and the Counties of Gloucestershire, Herefordshire and Worcestershire, and was in 1803 commanded by Lt General, The Duke of Cumberland.
3. Bute Lieutenancy Papers
4. Gazetted 13 December 1803
5. *Cambrian* 23 March 1804
6. District Inspector of Volunteers
7. *Cambrian* 30 March 1804
8. Naval Impress Service or Press Gang
9. *Cambrian* 20 April 1804
10. *Cambrian* 18 May 1804
11. *Cambrian* 1 June 1804
12. *Cambrian* 31 August 1804
13. *Gloucester Journal* 19 October 1803
14. *Cambrian* 12 October 1804
15. *Cambrian* 14 December 1804
16. *Cambrian* 8 February 1804
17. *Cambrian* 31 May 1805
18. *Cambrian* 27 November 1807
19. *Cambrian* 27 May 1808

70

Medal, Cardiff Volunteer Artillery,
1804.
[J L Balmer, TD]

20. *Cambrian* 24 June 1804
21. *Cambrian* 22 June 1804
22. *Cambrian* 12 October 1804
23. *Cambrian* 31 May 1805
24. *Cambrian* 14 June 1805
25. *Cambrian* 5 June 1807
26. *Cambrian* 13 November 1807
27. Willson, C James, *A View of the Volunteer Army of Great Britain*, 1806.
28. *Cambrian* 6 April 1804
29. *Cambrian* 25 May 1804
30. *Cambrian* 7 September 1804
31. PRO, HO Internal Defence Vol X11X & quoted by Fortescue J W,
     County Lieutenancies and the Army, 1803-14. p.116
32. *Cambrian* 31 May 1805
33. *Cambrian* 30 October 1807
34. *Cambrian* 3 June 1808
35. *Cambrian* 8 February 1805
36. *Cambrian* 8 February 1805
37. *Cambrian* 19 April 1805
38. *Cambrian* 11 October 1805
39. *Cambrian* 7 August 1807
40. *Hereford Journal* 16 November 1803
41. *Cambrian* 22 March 1804
42. *Cambrian* 20 April 1804
43. *Cambrian* 27 April 1804
44. *Cambrian* 25 May 1804
45. *Cambrian* 8 June 1804

46. *Cambrian* 15 June 1804
47. *Cambrian* 20 June 1804
48. *Cambrian* 12 October 1804
49. *Cambrian* 19 April 1805
50. *Cambrian* 17 May 1805
51. *Cambrian* 9 November 1807
52. *Hereford Journal* 16 November 1803
53. *Cambrian* 30 March 1804
54. *Cambrian* 25 May 1804
55. *Cambrian* 8 June 1804
56. *Cambrian* 7 December 1804
57. The Pembrokeshire Independent Yeomanry Cavalry
58. *Cambrian* 7 June 1805
59. *Cambrian* 14 June 1805
60. *Cambrian* 23 August 1805
61. *Cambrian* 9 May 1806
62. *Cambrian* 5 June 1807
63. *Cambrian* 3 June 1808
64. *Cambrian* 31 August 1808
65. *Cambrian* 19 October 1804
66. *Cambrian* 17 May 1805
67. *Cambrian* 31 May 1805
68. *Cambrian* 13 November 1807
69. *Cambrian* 27 May 1808
70. *Cambrian* 10 June 1808
71. *Cambrian* 10 June 1808
72. *Cambrian* 21 September 1808
73. Records of Major J L Balmer, TD.

Chapter 8
THE LOCAL MILITIA, 1808-16

The Local Militia Act [1] which became law on 30 June 1808, swept away, with the exception of yeomanry cavalry and a few isolated corps of artillery and infantry volunteers, a volunteer force which had grown so large and cumbersome as to be almost unmanageable from a military standpoint. It had tied up within its ranks a large proportion of the nation's fittest and most useful manpower, protected by volunteer privileges from the demands of the militia ballot and regular army recruiters. The creation of a more malleable force of Local Militia prompted the historian Fortescue to write :

Two hundred thousand men who could be compelled to undergo training and to do as they were told were substituted for an uncertain number who after great expense to the Country, still claimed the glorious privilege of doing as they pleased. The gain to the country was enormous; and as a natural consequence, a large proportion of the Regular Army was released for service beyond the sea.[2]

Not to be confused with the Regular or County Militia [3] (which at that time was embodied and serving outside the county on garrison duty) a Local Militiaman, whether recruited voluntarily or selected by ballot, was required to serve for four years. No substitutes were allowed, but a loophole was left open to men in certain categories, who could, on payment of a fine of between £10 and £30 gain exemption for a period of two years.

Where enforcement of the Local Militia ballot was necessary in order to complete the numbers required, it was applied to men between the ages of 18 and 30 years, who in addition to being compelled to attend a period of annual training, could, in the event of rebellion or invasion, be marched with their regiment to any part of Great Britain.

In the ordinary course of events, Local Militiamen were not required to serve outside the boundaries of their own or neighbouring counties. In those districts the Lords Lieutenant were empowered to use them in aid of civil power for a period of up to 14 days. Men serving in the new force were actively encouraged to enlist in the militia and the line, at any time other than the period in the year selected for Local Militia training.

Local Militia regiments were organised along the same lines as the County Militia regiments, with a proportion of the regimental staff on permanent (constant) pay. In the first instance the annual training period was set at a period not exceeding 28 days, but was later reduced in the interests of economy.

In July 1808, the commandants of the various Glamorgan Infantry Volunteer units received a circular letter from the War Secretary, requesting they inform the Clerk of the General Meetings of the Lieutenancy by 1 August, or within fourteen days thereof, of the number and rank of persons then serving in their corps who were willing to voluntarily transfer their services into the new force in order that the Local Militia Act could be put into execution. [4] In Glamorgan, the response was more than favourable, the required numbers being completed almost entirely by volunteers transferring their services en masse. The quota required from the county was to be six times the county militia quota, taking into account existing Yeomanry Cavalry or other volunteers still serving. A figure of 2,418 privates is given in the *Cambrian*, which numbers were to be divided amongst three regiments numbering not less than 700 and not more than 1200 as far as circumstances would permit. [5]

The first meeting of the Lieutenancy of the county for carrying into execution the terms of the Act was held at Pyle early in October 1808 [6] - somewhat late in the day, when one takes into account the fact that during the second week in September, the commanding officers of the various volunteer corps had received letters from the King, accepting the services of their units as part of the new Glamorgan Local Militia [7]; furthermore, those volunteers that had stood down on 23 September were to continue on the following day as components of the three new regiments of Local Militia. Presumably the October meeting was convened to finalise what had already been accomplished and to discuss any future requirements under the Act.

The Glamorgan Local Militia quota was divided into three regiments, viz:

The Eastern Regiment	- Lt Colonel Rowley Lascelles
The Central Regiment	- Lt Colonel Price
The Western Regiment	- Lt Colonel John Llewelyn (Penllergaer)

In November 1809, the *Cambrian* tells us that in September of the previous year 2,467 volunteers had transferred into the Local Militia, but that at the time of reporting, the Eastern, Central and Western regiments were respectively 31, 33 and 30 private men short on their establishments. It is therefore almost certain that the Local Militia ballot was enforced to make up the required numbers.

At first, service in the Local Militia seemed to those involved to be little different, and somewhat less demanding than service with the old Infantry Volunteer corps and many undoubtedly transferred in order to preserve their immunity from the main Militia Ballot. As time progressed, however, the Local Militia became less popular. The men missed the compactness and conviviality of the old volunteer units and the regulations governing them as Local Militiamen made them feel more like 'pressed men' and, consequently, few chose to re-engage when their four year stint was ended in 1812.

Unlike the Local Militia regiments of some counties, the regiments of Glamorgan were comparatively problem free. In some regiments a great deal of trouble was experienced over the payment of certain allowances, desertions were frequent and near mutiny not uncommon. Even the commanding officers of Local Militia were somewhat taken aback when, in December 1809, they found themselves required to insure the arms, accoutrements and clothing held on behalf of their regiments. It was made clear to them that, in the event of the loss of the whole, or part, by fire or other cause, they personally would be responsible to the government for making good the value. At this date also, the government, in pursuance of economies, reduced the numbers of Local Militia non-commissioned officers on constant pay, the unfortunate corporals being deprived of both pay and jobs when they were informed that their services were no longer required.

Fortescue opines that the government was at this stage finding the Local Militia to be a more troublesome and costly venture than had at first been anticipated.

Insufficient of its numbers were willing to consider transferring their services into the county militia and line, and doubts were expressed as to its value even in limited local and home defence, as the force did not devote as much time to training as had its volunteer predecessors. In March 1811, the number of days training was reduced from 21 to 14 days per annum, with the exception of the recruits who would train for 21 days and assemble one week ahead of the main body. That decision did nothing to improve the morale of what remained of Local Militia permanent staff or increase the overall efficiency of any regiment.

The year 1812 saw large numbers leave the force, they being the volunteers who had voluntarily transferred their services in 1808 and had, by that date, completed the four year engagement. The result was that almost overnight the Local Militia regiments were reduced to bodies of unwilling and untrained recruits, selected by enforcement of the ballot in order to maintain the regiments at the established strength.

As had been the case in the old volunteer corps, the spirit and enthusiasm of each regiment depended much upon the quality of, and interest shown by the officers. In that respect, Glamorgan appears to have been fortunate as the Inspection Reports of the period are most encouraging. In 1813, elements of the force were authorised to volunteer to serve outside their counties on garrison duty. As will be seen, there was some favourable response to that call from the Glamorgan regiments.

The Local Militia continued to be raised in the county and trained annually up to the year 1815. In May 1816, a Bill [8] to suspend the Local Militia ballot was passed. Thereafter enrolment ceased, and the force, never again to be revived, passed on into the pages of history.[9]

All three Glamorgan regiments wore a red jacket with blue facings.

The East Glamorgan Regiment of Local Militia, 1808-15

The regiment commenced its service on 24 September 1808, and was at that stage mainly made up of companies of volunteers who had transferred their services from the East Glamorgan Regiment of Volunteer Infantry. It first assembled for training under the command of Lt Colonel John Price on 20 May 1809, with Cardiff providing the venue for that 14 day period.

On Monday last the Eastern Glamorgan Regiment of Local Militia commanded by Lt Colonel Price were inspected at Cardiff by Colonel Madden. The Regiment was only out 14 days, yet the advanced state of their discipline in that short period, notwithstanding the unfavourable weather, reflects great credit on the Commander. The Men behaved remarkably well, and on their dismissal, departed in good order to their respective homes. [10]

The Regiment assembled again in Cardiff in June 1810 [11], May 1811 and June 1812. Following their 1812, inspection Major General Browne in General Orders stated:

> Major General Browne has great satisfaction in expressing his approbation and thanks to Lt Colonel Price for the very excellent formation and steadiness under arms of the Eastern Glamorgan Regiment of Local Militia. He requests Colonel Bassett and the Officers will also accept his thanks for their attention and readiness this day in the Field, which contributed to the correctness of the movements.[12]

The man who really deserved mention for whipping the regiment into shape was Sergeant Major William Wynn, as on his efficiency and that of his permanent staff NCOs depended as always the success or failure of the regiment's short period of annual training. As in previous years the Regiment received the thanks of the townspeople of Cardiff for the exemplary conduct of the men, particularly when off duty.

In 1813, the Regiment assembled in Cardiff for training in June and was inspected by Major General Sir William Cockburn on the 19th of the month.

> They performed the different manoeuvres with such precision as to merit warm encomium.[13]

The last assembly of the regiment for training took place on 28 March 1814. In the following year it stood down and was shortly thereafter disbanded.[14]

Cross belt plate, East Glamorgan Local Militia, 1808-16. [Cyfarthfa Castle Museum, Merthyr Tydfil]

Officers serving in 1811 were:

Lt Colonel Commandant John Price	24 September 1808
Lt Colonel John Bassett	24 September 1808
Major Daniel Jones	24 September 1808
Captain Windham Lewis Jnr	24 September 1808
Captain William Meyrick	24 September 1808
Captain Evan Samuel	24 September 1808
Captain John Jones	24 September 1808
Captain Thomas Rees	24 September 1808
Captain Whitlock Nicholl	24 September 1808
Captain Thomas Williams	6 May 1809
Captain Thomas Newte	22 May 1809
Captain William Davis	9 August 1811
Captain Henry Hollier	9 August 1811
1st Lieut David Hopkins	24 September 1808
1st Lieut Benjamin Thomas	24 September 1808
1st Lieut Thomas Thomas	24 September 1808
1st Lieut Richard Mumford	24 September 1808
1st Lieut Thomas Gardiner	24 September 1808
1st Lieut George Bird	17 May 1809
1st Lieut W Jacob	17 May 1809
1st Lieut G E Aubrey	17 May 1809
1st Lieut Evan Davies	17 May 1809
1st Lieut W Vachell	17 May 1809
2nd Lieut Thomas Evans	24 September,1808
2nd Lieut Worley Birch	6 May, 1809
2nd Lieut Capel Beadles	17 May, 1809
2nd Lieut John Harris	17 May, 1809
2nd Lieut Charles Vachell	17 May, 1809
2nd Lieut John Williams	19 August, 1811
Captain & Adjutant Edward Sterling	30 August, 1811
Quartermaster Henry Lewis	9 August, 1811
Surgeon B Grover	24 September, 1808

Central Glamorgan Regiment of Local Militia, 1808-15

The Regiment commenced its service on 24 September 1808, and was made up mainly of companies of ex-volunteers who had transferred their services from Rowley Lascelles' Glamorgan Riflemen and William Vaughan's Prince of Wales's Fuzileers. It first assembled for training in Swansea on 21 April 1809, for a 28 day period, and under the command of Lt Colonel Lascelles.

The Central Glamorgan Local Militia commanded by Colonel Lascelles completed their 28 days of permanent duty yesterday, and having deposited their Arms and Cothing were dismissed. At the evening parade, the Colonel thanked the men for their conduct

Bicorne hat, officer, Central Glamorgan Local Militia, c1808.
[National Museum of Wales; Welsh Folk Museum]

whilst they had been under his command, and after wishing them health and happiness, took his leave until next year amidst hearty cheers from the whole Corps. [15]

Being drawn from both eastern and western parts of the county, the Central Regiment also used Cardiff and Cowbridge as places of assembly, the 1810 training commencing at Cardiff on 24 April for a period of twenty days. The town was also the place of assembly in 1811 when training commenced on 15 May. Later, the regiment moved on to Cowbridge in which town it was quartered at the end of the 14 day training period.

The General Meeting of the Lieutenancy holden for fixing the place and period for assembling the Central Regiment of Local Militia of the County resolved that the said Regiment under the command of Lt Colonel Lascelles will assemble at Cardiff at 10 o'clock in the forenoon of the 15th May next for 14 days annual training and exercise during the present year, exclusive of the days of arriving or departure from the place of assembly. [16]

The Central Glamorgan Regiment commanded by Colonel Lascelles were dismissed from their permanent duty yesterday at Cowbridge. This fine Corps supported its former exalted reputation and deserves the most honourable mention. They were inspected on Saturday by Colonel Molyneaux [17] and obtained his decided approbation. [18]

The 1812 training terminated in Cardiff on 19 May during which period the regiment was inspected by Major General Browne. As usual, the conduct of the men was both regular and exemplary, and all received a glowing report:

> Major General Browne and the Officers under his command feel great pleasure in an opportunity of expressing his thanks to Lt Colonel Lascelles and the Officers under his command for the very military appearance of the Central Glamorgan Regiment of Local Militia this day in the Field. Their Dress, correctness and quickness with which they performed their movements was highly creditable to every department of the regiment, and their firing also exceeded his expectations. Major General Browne will not fail to report the conduct of the Corps in the strong terms they merit. [19]

In 1813, the Regiment was drawn out for 14 days training commencing 13 May. Major General Sir William Cockburn inspected them on the 26th and was as strong with his praise as had been Major General Browne in the previous year.

On assembling in Cardiff on the 25 March 1814, the men were informed that a number could volunteer for extended service guarding prisoners of war outside the county boundary.

> When the nature of the Act was fully explained to them by their Commandant and Lt Colonel Bruce, 200 men immediately volunteered for the Stapleton Prison Guard.[20] To the great credit of the Officers of this well appointed Regiment, they volunteered with one exception, although many of them hold situations so responsible as to make six weeks duty a personal inconvenience. This Regiment is composed principally of Balloted Men, nearly the whole of the members serving for the four preceding years having been discharged. [21]

As far as is known the Regiment did not assemble for training in 1815, but stood down and was disbanded in the course of that year.

Officers serving in the Central Regiment in 1811 were:

Lt Colonel Commandant Rowley Lascelles	24 September 1808
Lt Colonel William Vaughan	24 September 1808
Major John Edwards	24 September 1808
Captain J.J.Bassett	24 September 1808
Captain J.W.Barton	24 September 1808
Captain John Miles	24 September 1808
Captain Robert Savours	24 September 1808
Captain R.H.Dingley	24 September 1808
Captain Samuel Waterman	22 April 1809
Captain Christopher Perkins	22 April 1809
Captain Thomas Grove	12 October 1809
Captain Morgan Davies	17 May 1810
Captain S P Howell	22 April 1811
1st Lieut Griffith Griffiths	24 September 1808

1st Lieut William Jones	24 September 1808
1st Lieut David Jenkins	24 September 1808
1st Lieut Robert Falkner	23 April 1809
1st Lieut Edward Jenkins	27 September 1810
1st Lieut George Roberts	22 April 1811
Captain & Adjutant R R Roberts	24 September 1808
Quartermaster John Ballard	24 September 1808

The Regiment was short of six Lieutenants and eight 2nd Lieutenants in consequence of which several of the companies had no officer other than a captain.

Centrepiece of the Regimental Colour, West Glamorgan Local Militia, 1808-16.   [Swansea Museum]

West Glamorgan Regiment of Local Militia, 1808-15

The regiment commenced its service on 24 September 1808, and in similar manner to the Eastern and Central regiments was mainly composed of ex-Volunteers who, in this instance, had transferred their services from John Llewelyn's 1st or West Glamorgan Volunteer Infantry and Lockwood's Fforest Riflemen.

The Regiment first assembled at its Swansea Headquarters for 28 days training on 22 May 1809. On 4 June, it paraded with others to celebrate the King's Birthday :

> The Anniversary of our venerable and well beloved Sovereign was celebrated in Swansea on Monday with every demonstration of loyalty attachment. The bells rang nearly all day, and the Ship's in harbour displayed their Colours. Royal Salutes were fired by the *Eliza* Tender and *Morriston* Armed Brig. The Western Glamorgan Local Militia and the Swansea Cavalry fired three capital volleys. [22]

During the training period the regiment was inspected by Colonel Madden with excellent results. On the last day of training,

> Lt Colonel Jenkins (acting in the absence of the Commanding Officer, who was suddenly called out to Hereford to preside at a Court Martial)[23], publicly thanked the men for their praiseworthy conduct in the Field, as well as in Quarters, and no Corps, we can with truth assert, more justly merited an encomium. In the evening, Lt Colonel Llewelyn gave an elegant Ball and Supper to his Officers and numerous principal inhabitants at the Town Hall. [24]

On the 28 May 1810, the regiment assembled in Swansea for its second annual training period and, as in the previous year, joined in celebrations to celebrate the King's 72nd Birthday.

> The Military, both Infantry and Cavalry fired several excellent volleys, and the *Morriston* Brig, and the *Minerva*, Captain Vidal, fired salutes in honour of the day. [25]

During the ceremonies, the Adjutant of the West Glamorgan, Captain William Jones, was thrown from his rather excitable horse and suffered a fractured leg. Prior to dismissal the regiment was inspected by General Dyot who after witnessing it manoeuvres and live firing practice was pleased to declare,

> that the distinguished appearance of the Regiment, its state of discipline, the steadiness of all Ranks in the field movements, the general good order and the particular attention to dress of the men merited the strongest praise he could offer. [26]

The West Glamorgan next assembled in Swansea on the 5 June 1811, prior to which the following notice was distributed in the county.

> The West Glamorgan Regiment of Local Militia, by permission of HRH The Prince

Button, officers pattern,
Glamorgan Local Militia,
1808-16.

Regent, and under author-ity of the Lieutenancy of the County will assemble at Swansea on the 5th of next month, and on the 6th commence their duty for 14 days and be dismissed on the 20th. The Officers, Non-Commissioned Officers, Drummers and Privates must be at Headquarters at the time above mentioned, and under the Regulations of Government, no leave of absence can be granted during the period of assembly except in cases of the most urgent necessity. The Recruits belonging to the Regiment who have not before joined, will be at Head-quarters seven days prior to the Regiment going on duty. [27]

During the training the regiment was inspected by General Crosby with the usual excellent results.

The 1812 and 1813 training periods com-menced on 9 June, the venue, as in previous years, being Swansea. Inspected by Major General Browne in 1812 and by Major General Sir William Cockburn in 1813, the West Glamorgan showed it had lost none of its zeal or proficiency and again received much praise for its exemplary behaviour in the town during training.

Their steady and well directed Fire, and the correctness with which they executed their different movements in the Field this morning are equally honourable to the attention and the ability of the Officers as well as the good conduct of the Men. [28]

The Regiment assembled for the last time in 1815, but stood down and was disbanded during the course of the year.

Officers serving in 1811 were:

Lt Colonel Commandant John Llewelyn	24 September 1808
Lt Colonel R H Jenkins	24 September 1808
Major Thomas Lockwood	24 September 1808
Major M P Traherne	24 September 1808
Captain Josef May	24 September 1808
Captain Thomas Hobbes	24 September 1808
Captain Thomas Leyson	24 September 1808
Captain John Voss	24 September 1808
Captain Edward Hawkins	24 September 1808
Captain David Long	24 September 1808
Captain Thomas Jackson	24 September 1808
Captain John Jeffries	24 September 1808
Captain John Minshull	24 September 1808

Captain Thomas Morgan	13 June 1810
Captain Samuel Hawkins	13 June 1810
Captain Lewis Thomas	12 July 1811
1st Lieut Solomon Bowen	24 September 1808
1st Lieut David Powell	24 September 1808
1st Lieut Thomas Eaves	24 September 1808
1st Lieut W Bevan	24 September 1808
1st Lieut John Grove	24 September 1808
1st Lieut T L Martin	24 September 1808
1st Lieut W Baker	16 July 1809
1st Lieut Thomas Sleasby	16 July 1809
1st Lieut W Richards	28 February 1810
1st Lieut Robert Harwood	18 May 1810
1st Lieut Thomas Thomas	16 March 1811
1st Lieut William Howells	16 March 1811
1st Lieut Thomas Burnell	16 March 1811
2nd Lieut Robert Harwood	24 September 1808
2nd Lieut W Williams	24 September 1808
2nd Lieut David Davies	24 September 1808
2nd Lieut John Williams	12 September 1810
Captain & Adjutant William Jones	24 September 1808
Quartermaster Thomas Llewelyn	24 September 1808
Surgeon Leyson Rees	17 May 1811

The Regimental Colour: The Regimental Colour of the West Glamorgan Regiment of Local Militia has survived thanks to the care devoted to it by John Llewelyn and his successors. In later years, the colour was placed in the care of the Royal Institution of South Wales at Swansea, in whose custody it remains. Of the few Welsh Local Militia colours which have survived the passage of over 170 years, the West Glamorgan colour stands out as being the best preserved. It is hoped that its present custodians are aware of its value in terms of Glamorgan military history, and that they, unlike other authorities in the Principality, will take such steps as are necessary to see it preserved fo the future.

NOTES
1. Act 48 Geo 11.c.3.
2. Fortescue.J.W. *History of the British Army*,Vol 1V,p.183.
3. The Royal Glamorgan Militia.
4. *Cambrian* 22 July 1808.
5. *Cambrian* 23 September 1808.
6. *Cambrian* 7 October1808.
7. *Cambrian* 16 September 1808.
8. Act 56 Geo 111,c.3. May 21st, 1816.
9. Orders in Council were made annually under the Act up to 1832 to continue the suspension of the Local Militia Ballot. In 1873, the Act was finally repealed as obsolete.

Shoulder belt plate, West Glamorgan Local Militia, 1808-16.
[Dr J Carey Hughes]

10. *Cambrian* 16 June 1809.
11. *Cambrian* 8 June 1810.
12. *Cambrian* 5 June 1812.
13. *Cambrian* 25 June 1813.
14. *Cambrian* 11 March 1814
15. *Cambrian* 21 April 1809 & 19 May 1809.
16. *Cambrian* 1 April 1811.
17. Inspecting Field Officer and Commanding Officer of the East Monmouthshire Regt of Local Militia.
18. *Cambrian* 13 May 1811.
19. *Cambrian* 22 May 1812.
20. Stapleton Gaol, Bristol which in those days housed a large number of prisoners of war.
21. *Cambrian* 1 April 1814.
22. *Cambrian* 9 June 1809.
23. The Trial by Court Martial of a Herefordshire Local Militia NCO.
24. *Cambrian* 23 June 1809.
25. *Cambrian* 8 June 1810.
26. *Cambrian* 22 June 1810.
27. *Cambrian* 11 May 1811.
28. *Cambrian* 25 June 1813.

Chapter 9
Independent Corps of Glamorgan Yeomanry Cavalry, 1808-13

The stand down of the infantry volunteers and the formation of three large regiments of Local Militia in September 1808 resulted in the two troops of the Swansea Cavalry, together with the Fairwood and Cardiff Troops of Gentlemen and Yeomanry, becoming the only volunteer units remaining in service within the county boundaries. They were commanded respectively by Captain Hughes, Captain Sir Gabriel Powell and Captain John Wood. The activities of the three corps during this period were confined to local training and periods of annual permanent duty. In 1808, the Swansea troops, having been dismissed from their permanent duty on 9 June, were described as:

> This excellent Corps is composed of individuals chiefly in the most respected situations in life, and as a military body are an honour to the cause in which they are engaged. [1]

The Fairwood troop came out twice during the year, the first commencing on 16 September and the second in November. Commenting on the latter event, the *Cambrian* stated:

> The Fairwood Corps of Cavalry commanded by Sir Gabriel Powell completed their term of Permanent Duty in Swansea on Wednesday last with much credit, as well as for their orderly and soldierlike conduct, and for their careful attention to improve in discipline and efficiency.[2]

In Cardiff, the local troop had trained in May and exercised with the Usk Volunteer Infantry of Monmouthshire which was on temporary garrison duty in the town. Colonel Madden on inspecting the troop expressed himself eminently satisfied with their general state of efficiency. After the June 1809 inspection, the same Inspecting Field Officer was moved to state that the troop had more the appearance of veteran soldiers than Yeomanry and that he would report them as being fit to serve alongside the Regiments of the Line.[3]

Moving on to West Glamorgan, Madden inspected the Fairwood and Swansea troops on 19 June and expressed himself well pleased with their efficiency and progress. By 1810, Colonel Molyneaux, a retired regular officer and commanding officer of the East Monmouthshire Local Militia, had been appointed Inspecting Field Officer for South Wales. He inspected the Yeomanry Cavalry troops twice in that year, the Cardiff troop on 16 April and 21 September, and the Fairwood and Swansea troops on 17 April and 22 September. On each occasion he expressed himself satisfied with their general efficiency. In June the three West Glamorgan troops joined with the Local Militia in celebrating the King's Birthday.

The military, both Infantry and Cavalry, fired several excellent volleys, and the *Morriston* Brig and the *Minerva*, Captain Vidal, fired Royal Salutes in honour of the day. [4]

The round of training and inspection continued throughout 1811 and 1812. In Swansea, the single Fairwood troop and the two Swansea troops had drawn closer and were acting more or less as one body, but in Cardiff, the local troop remained quite independent. Still commanded by Captain John Wood (his son John Wood Jnr was a Lieutenant), its training was supervised by Sergeant John Culbert, an ex-regular cavalryman who was employed as Permanent Staff Instructor.

In 1813, the government, in a move aimed at increasing the efficiency of the Yeomanry Cavalry force, directed that the various small units within county and other district boundaries should unite to form Yeomanry corps of, ideally, six troops, or where this was not possible, units comprising no less than three troops. Thus (on paper at least) the three Glamorgan Yeomanry corps were united but, within an organisation sufficiently flexible to allow the three Captains Commandant a great deal of autonomy.

The Glamorgan Yeomanry Cavalry Corps, 1813-31

Although consolidated to form a Glamorgan Yeomanry corps of four troops, no record dated pre-1816 has been found which suggests that much effort was made to exercise the county Yeomanry as one corps. Such evidence as exists shows a merging of the Swansea troops and the Fairwood troop under the title 'Swansea and Fairwood Troops' but with the Cardiff troop continuing to act and train independently. In October 1816, discontent over the high price of bread, the truck system and low wages, resulted in a strike and mob violence in that part of South Wales best known today as the Heads of the Valleys. The action by workers resulted in a rapid shut down of every blast furnace between Merthyr Tydfil in Glamorgan and Llangyneidr in Breconshire and in Merthyr Tydfil, Josiah Guest, master of the Dowlais iron works was roughly handled by the mob and then besieged by rioters in Dowlais House. In fear of their lives the defenders of Dowlais House made use of firearms, killing one and injuring several of the attackers. Embodied by the order of the Lord Lieutenant on Friday, 18 October, the Cardiff troop and a detachment of the Swansea and Fairwood cavalry arrived in Merthyr Tydfil to assist 120 Officers and Men of the 55th Regiment [5] and the Permanent Staff of the Royal Glamorgan Light Infantry Militia. Not long after

86

A Private of the Cardiff Troop of Gentlemen and Yeomanry, c1810.
[From a watercolour commissioned by the author. Artist, M Chappell]

their arrival, the troops confronted a crowd estimated at about 8,000 outside the Castle Inn. Magistrates read the Riot Act, but the crowd refused to disperse. The magistrates then handed matters over to the Yeomanry who, to their credit, completed the task without any serious injury or loss of life.

On 21 October, the Swansea detachment were ordered into north Monmouthshire where, in conjunction with detachments of the Monmouthshire Yeomanry Cavalry, they were able to prevent the workers massing. Later, the Swansea Yeomen were active in the Newport district where their presence contributed greatly towards the preservation of good order and public safety. For their services during that difficult period, the Swansea and Fairwood troops received a commendation from the the Secretary of State, Lord Sidmouth.

In 1818, the uniform of the Glamorgan Troops of Yeomanry which, with its striking Light Cavalry Helmet or Tarleton had remained unchanged since 1803, was discarded in favour of a more up to date fashion which was intended to be worn as standard dress by all troops of the corps. The Swansea and Fairwood troops were the first to wear the new kit on assembling in Swansea for 8 days permanent duty on Monday, 16 November, 1818.

> The Men are newly dressed in Blue Jackets with white facings and grey pantaloons. They make a very handsome martial appearance, and their attention to duty as well as good conduct are exemplary as usual. [6]

The shako replaced the Tarleton and, in due course, the four troops of the Corps were similarly dressed and accoutred.

Officers of the Glamorgan Yeomanry Corps in 1819 were as follows:

Swansea Troop

Major Edward Hughes	Swansea	4 April 1814
Captain Robert Nelson Thomas	Swansea	26 July 1804
Captain Hugh Powell Watkins	Swansea	4 April 1814
Lt Herbert Edward Evans	Swansea	
Lt John Griffiths Hancorne	Bishopston	9 January 1817
Lt Rowland Hopkin	Bishopston	
Lt John Jones	Bishopston	
Cornet John Davies	Swansea	15 November 1818
Cornet Charles Collins	Swansea	
Adjutant George Harries	Swansea	24 December 1816
Quartermaster Simon Llewelyn	Swansea	
Quartermaster Richard Jones	Ilstone	
Surgeon John Davies	Swansea	10 January 1817
Surgeon Charles Sylvester	Swansea	10 January 1817

CENTRAL
Glamorgan Yeomanry.

To the Gentlemen and Yeomen of Cowbridge, Bridgend, and Margam, and their respective Neighbourhoods.

A Commission having been directed to issue for raisin a Troop of Volunteer Cavalry, to be called the "CENTRAL GLAMORGAN YEOMANRY," and to be commanded by Mr. NICHOLL, of Merthyrmawr; all Persons desirous of serving in the said Troop, are requested to send in their Names for Enrolment, either to Mr. NICHOLL, at Merthyrmawr; Mr. LLEWELLYN, Postmaster, Cowbridge; or to Mr. JOSEPH WILLIAMS, Savings Bank, Bridgend.

N. B. The Number of the Troop being limited, a I there being an advantage, from early Enrolment, in obtai ing a .owances, it is requested that those who are desirous or serving, will lose no time in signifying their intentions.

Merthyrmawr, August, 1820.

PRINTED BY R. LLOYD, HIGH-STREET, CARDIFF.

Printed notice relating to the Central Glamorgan Yeomanry, 1820.
[P McLachlan, DL & Glamorgan County Records Office]

Fairwood Troop
Lt Stephen Bowen Jones   Swansea   14 December 1818
Quartermaster John Morgan   Swansea

Cardiff Troop
Captain Whitlock Nicholl   21 May 1819
Vacancies for one Lieutenant and one Cornet.

The Swansea & Fairwood troops came out on Permanent Duty in Swansea in November 1819 and were dismissed on the 23rd of the month.

Much to the credit of this truly respectable Corps, the muster was particularly good and their conduct meritorious. [7]

As previously stated, no record has been found which mentions the presentation of Troop Standards to either the Fairwood or Swansea troops of Gentlemen and Yeomanry, but it is more than likely that such distinctions were carried. The *Cambrian,* reporting on the Proclamation Ceremony in Swansea on the Accession of King George IV, in February 1820, states:

Troop Standard of the Cardiff Troop of Yeomanry Cavalry, c1806.
National Museum of Wales: Welsh Folk Museum.

Standard of the Central Glamorgan Yeomanry, 1820.
[P McLachlan, DL]

On that morning the Corporation preceded by a Detachment of the Swansea Cavalry, dismounted with Band of Music and Colours were followed by a number of respectable inhabitants in procession. [8]

Perhaps the "Colours" referred to were the standards of the Swansea and Fairwood troops of Yeomanry Cavalry. Permanent duty for the three west Glamorgan troops commenced on 29 May and extended over 8 days. The establishment for the year 1820 was 160 non-commissioned Officers and private men divided as follows:

1st Troop - Captain Robert Nelson Thomas   - 60
2nd Troop - Captain Hugh Powell Watkins   - 51
3rd Troop - Captain Herbert Edward Evans   - 56
with seven in excess of the authorised establishment.

The Cardiff Troop - Captain Whitlock Nicholl returned 46 rank and file in 1820 and three non-commissioned officers are mentioned, viz: Sergeant William Bradley (Cardiff), Sergeant William Phillips (Monmouthshire) and Sergeant Rowland Hopkins (Cadoxton, near Barry).

Henry Knight Esquire Vice Lieutenant of the County of Glamorgan by the authority of The Most Honorable John Marquess of Bute Earl of Dumfries and Earl of Windsor Viscount Montjoy of the Isle of Weight Baron Mount Stuart de Wortley Baron Cardiff of Cardiff Castle Lord Lieutenant and Custos Rotulorum of the said County of Glamorgan To all whom these presents may concern sends greeting

Know ye that by virtue and in pursuance of the several acts of Parliament passed and now in force relating to the Volunteers of Great Britain I do by these presents constitute and appoint John Nicholl of Merthyr Mawr in the said County of Glamorgan Esquire to be Captain Commandant in the Central Glamorgan Troop of Gentlemen and Yeomanry Cavalry And I do hereby give and grant full power and authority to the said John Nicholl to command and take his rank accordingly. He is therefore carefully and diligently to discharge the Duty of Captain Commandant by exercising and well disciplining the inferior Officers, non-commissioned Officers, and private men of the said Troop And I do hereby command them to obey him as their Captain Commandant And the said John Nicholl is to observe and follow such orders and directions from time to time as he shall receive from the Lord Lieutenant of the County of Glamorgan, the Vice Lieutenant of the said County of Glamorgan or any other his superior Officer according to the Directions of the several acts of Parliament now in force, and in pursuance of the Trust reposed in him. Given under my hand and seal this nineteenth day of August in the year of our Lord one thousand Eight hundred and Twenty.

Hn. Knight.

The Commission of John Nicholl as Captain Commandant of the Central Glamorgan Yeomanry Cavalry, 1820.
[P McLachlan, DL & the Glamorgan County Records Office]

As previously mentioned, the new style uniform selected for wear by the Glamorgan Yeomanry had made its appearance in Swansea in 1818. The Cardiff troop received its issue in July 1820 and first appeared thus clothed at a church parade.

> On Sunday last the Cardiff Troop of Yeomanry Cavalry under the command of Captain W Nicholls assembled in their new Full Dress Uniforms and attended Divine Service at Cardiff Church with the Staff of the Royal Glamorgan Militia. In the afternoon, they made their first appearance mounted since the introduction of Hussar Saddles and Accoutrements. In justice to the Gentlemen composing the Troop it was observed that the respectable military appearance and the excellence of their Horses,would have done justice to any Regiment of the Line. We understand that it is the intention of the Troop honouring Cowbridge with their presence on Tuesday next.[9]

"Tuesday next" in fact marked the commencement of 8 days permanent duty in Cowbridge. In October, the troop came together again for six days training in Cardiff.

The unsettled state of the working class in the industrial districts of South Wales prompted the Lord Lieutenant to send a memorandum to a number of influential gentlemen in the county.

> The Lord Lieutenant and the Lieutenancy having deemed it expedient to increase the Volunteer Cavalry Force of Glamorganshire by the raising of two additional Troops, one in the Central part and the other at Llantrisant and its neighbourhood. It is conceived that the inhabitants of these districts may derive benefit from the measure, while the inconvenience will rest solely on those who personally engage in it. (10)

The Central Glamorgan Troops of Yeomanry Cavalry

Amongst the additional troops of Yeomanry Cavalry raised in 1820 were two troops of Central Glamorgan Cavalry whose acceptance for service by the King was communicated to the Marquis of Bute in a letter dated 17 July 1820. Raised by John Nicholl, Esq, of Merthyr Mawr, near Bridgend, the establishment of each troop was set at: 1 captain, 1 lieutenant, 1 cornet, 1 quartermaster, 2 sergeants, 2 corporals, 1 trumpeter and 52 private men. The officers of the 1st Central Troop were:

Captain John Nicholl of Merthyr Mawr   19 August 1820
Lt Benjamin Hall
Cornet Lloyd Vaughan Williams
Quartermaster Richard Burnell of Newton

The numbers required for the 1st Troop were rapidly completed, in consequence of which John Nicholl went on to raise a second. That this augmentation was acceptable to the King was repeated in a letter received by John

Nicholl from the Vice-Lieutenant of the county dated 2 September and which included the new establishment for the Central troops effective from 30 August, 1820, viz: 1 captain, 2 lieutenants, 1 cornet, 1 quartermaster, 5 sergeants, 5 corporals, 1 trumpeter, 100 privates.

Although John Nicholl had no difficulty in raising non-commissioned officers and men, the same was not true in respect of officers. It was not until 5 September 1822, that an additional lieutenant was found, on which date the position was filled by Christopher Rice Mansell Talbot of Margam. The catchment area for the Central troops was spread widely across the Vale of Glamorgan, hence the corps was divided into four sub-divisions. Of these, the eastern sub-division was allowed to assemble separately for most purposes other than permanent duty.

Non-commissioned officers of the Central troops in 1820 were:

Orderly Room Sgt & Clerk	John (Joseph) Williams of Bridgend
Orderly Room Corporal	Craddock Burnel of Newton
Sergeant	Evan Morgan of Tydraw, Cornelly
	(West Centre Sub-Div)
Corporal	John Williams of Sker
	(West Centre Sub-Div)
Sergeant	Morgan Bevan of Crugwallt
	(West Sub-Div)
Corporal	David Edwards of Gelliofid
	(West Sub-Div)
Sergeant	Thomas Evans of Cefncarfan
	(East Centre Sub-Div)
Corporal	John David of Cefncribwr
	(East Centre Sub-Div)
Sergeant	W Thomas of Penlline
	(East Sub-Div)
Corporal	James Hiscock of Cowbridge
	(East Sub-Div)
Farrier	R.Roberts of Margam
Trumpeter	E.Lewis of Cornelly
Drill Sergeant	John Harris

Of the above, only two appear to have had previous military experience, gained when serving as sergeants in the Glamorgan Local Militia 1808-16.

The Central troops first assembled for training on 19 October 1820, which event was the first of five training periods to be held on Ogmore Down before the year ended. Arms and ammunition for their use arrived in Cardiff on the 27 November and were shortly afterwards handed over to John Nicholl by the Adjutant of the Royal Glamorgan Militia. The invoice lists, among other things, 112 pistols with swivels and rammers, 112 sabres with buff leather sword knots, 12 carbines with bayonets, scabbards and rammers.

Officer, Central Glamorgan Yeomanry Cavalry, c1825.
[From a pen and ink drawing by M Chappell]

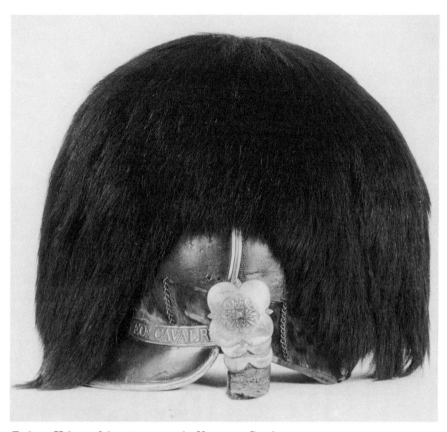

Tarleton Helmet of the pattern worn by Yeomanry Cavalry
and some Infantry Volunteer Corps.

A return dated 28 December 1820, gives the strength of the Central troops as 1 captain, 1 lieutenant and 112 rank and file.

The Llantrisant Troop of Yeomanry Cavalry

Also raised 1820, the Llantrisant Troop had as its Captain, Richard Fowler Rickards of Llantrisant House, the son of the Rev Robert Rickards, one time Vicar of Llantrisant. Only one other officer is listed in 1820, namely a Cornet Robert Hillier Rickards, the son of the Captain Commandant. Troop strength stood at 68 other ranks in 1821.

Uniform and Accoutrements of the Central Glamorgan Troops: As has been already stated, a standard form of dress was adopted for the Glamorgan

Yeomanry Corps - a uniform based upon that worn by the Light Dragoons of the day. Before proceeding to clothe his troops, John Nicholl sought advice from the Swansea Cavalry, probably in order to ensure some degree of standardisation. Fortunately, much of the documentation relating to the clothing transactions of the Central troops has been preserved in the Merthyr Mawr Papers, and therefore a fairly accurate description of the dress and accoutrements can be given.

Head-dress – Officers: Officers wore a black beaver cloth shako, bell-topped and similar in style to that worn by the 4th Light Dragoons. The headpiece was about 8" deep with a sunken leather top about 11" in diameter and it had a 2" band of silver oak leaf pattern lace around the top and a black silk binding at the bottom. Scalloped gilded scales were tied across the front under a gold bullion circle with black silver lining. At the sides, the scales were held in position by lionheads and a rich gold cap-line encircled the headpiece passing through a lionhead and ring on the side, then on around the wearers body, to hook up - the ends of the lines culminating in gold points. The shako had a black patent leather peak and chinstrap with a gilt plume holder supporting a full falling black plume of horsehair. On the front of the shako and within the bullion circle was worn the corps badge, namely the plumes, coronet and motto of the Prince of Wales in silver. In inclement weather, an oiled skin cover was worn. The cost of the shako was made up as follows:

Shako complete with scales, cockade and badge	£4 - 0 - 0
Cap-lines and ring	£3 - 0 - 0
Gilt plume holder	4 - 6
Black horsehair plume	6 - 0
Oiled skin cover	6 - 6
Total cost	£7 - 17 - 0 (£7.85)

Head-dress - The Quartermaster: The shako worn by the quartermaster (a warrant officer) was not quite so ornate as that worn by officers. It had a 2" band of silver lace around the top of the headpiece and a silver plated badge. Scales and other ornaments were made of brass, but the peak was bound with plated metal similar to the more ornate pattern. The cap-line is described as crimson and yellow with tassels. The plume, as for all ranks, was black horsehair. Total cost with oiled skin cover - £1-10-0 (£1.50)

Head-dress - Other Ranks: A plain bell topped shako of blue cloth with brass fittings and a black patent leather peak bound in white metal. The cap-lines were made of white cotton and the shako badge of plated metal. Total cost, with plume and oilskin cover was one guinea (£1.05).

Cap Foraging Undress - Officers: A blue foraging cap with silver lace band and black patent leather peak was worn by the officers. The men wore a worsted blue cloth cap with a white band, but peakless. The cost of the officers cap is given as 16s-6d (82p).

Uniform - Officers: The officers wore a short tailed coatee of plain blue cloth with a stand up collar faced in white. It had white lapels, buttoned back and three rows of silver regimental pattern buttons down the front. The skirts were short with white turnbacks and buttons with a short silver fringe at the back waist. The cuffs were pointed and faced with white cloth and a gold and a silver lancer girdle was worn around the waist. Silver bullion epaulettes were worn on each shoulder, the strap embellished with a silver regimental button at the point.

Overalls of blue-grey cloth with a double stripe of silver lace down each outside leg seam, black Wellington boots and gilded spurs completed the outfit

Accoutrements worn consisted of a black patent leather pouch with silver plumes, coronet and motto badge on the flap. The pouch was supported by a bleached leather pouch belt with silver point, buckle and slide.

A bleached leather waistbelt with plated furnishings and a small distinctive plate was worn which supported sword slings of similar material. Other items described on the invoices are :

A steel sabre with plain pipe back blade and steel scabbard at £3-13-6.

A cavalry sword knot, bleached leather strap and gold and crimson tassel at £1.

A black leather sabretache with silver lace and silver plumes ornament on the flap together with three supporting straps and buckles at £1-9-0.

Uniform - Other Ranks: Shakos and other accoutrements were purchased from Messers Hibbert & Hume of London, but the contract for the clothing, *ie,* a jacket and pantaloons was placed locally with David Major, tailor of Bridgend. He in turn, subcontracted to other tailors in the district. The specification describes jackets with three rows of buttons and of blue dragoon cloth. Overalls of grey twilled cloth strapped with cotton and leather on the inside. The cost - £3-5-0 (£3.25) per suit. Additionally, each man was supplied with a blue cloak with white collar, and a lancer girdle with three stripes of blue and two of buff, a combination which did not match those worn by the officers. Each man was also supplied with a six-round leather pouch, the flap decorated with the plumes badge in plated metal and a bleached leather pouch belt with white metal tip, buckle and slide. Sabres, 1797 stirrup hilted pattern with steel scabbards were together with sword knots supplied by the government.

Although the description given fits accurately the dress worn by the Central Troops and generally the dress of the others, there existed one or two minor differences. The buttons on the coatees for example were in no way standard. Those worn by the Central Troops carried the the plumes, coronet and motto device within a crowned belt inscribed 'Central Glamorgan'. Those of the Llantrisant Troop bore the letters 'LYC'. The badges worn on the shako were also different such as that worn by the Eastern Corps, the formation of which will be discussed later.

The Cardiff Troop assembled in Cardiff on 23 February 1821, for a period of training. The unit had vacancies and invited interested men to attend at the Adamstown Headquarters.

In April, Lloyd Vaughan Watkins was apppointed Cornet in the Central Troop and in June the Cardiff and Llantrisant Troops were inspected by the Lord Lieutenant. In July all the Troops participated in local celebrations to mark the Coronation of King George IV.

1823 saw Timothy Castles, late sergeant major of the 3rd Light Dragoons, appointed sergeant major to the Central corps. He took up residence at the corps headquarters, Bridgend and proved to be an excellent choice for the duties. As the Central Troops were not entitled to a sergeant major on the establishment, Sgt Major Castle's salary and expenses were met by John Nicholl of Merthyr Mawr. In 1824, John Nicholl proposed, after discussion with Captain Rickards of Llantrisant, that the Central and Llantrisant Corps be united with Mr Rickards as the Commandant. Under this proposal John Nichol and C.R.M. Talbot would remain as Captains of the two Central Glamorgan Troops. It was also agreed that Bridgend should be the headquarters and that Timothy Castles should remain as sergeant major. The plan received the blessing of both the Lord Lieutenant and the War Office. By August, the unification was complete with Richard Fowler Rickards as Major Commandant.

The state of the Glamorgan Yeomanry Corps in September 1824 was as follows:

Swansea and Fairwood Corps - 3 Troops - Major Hughes
Central Glamorgan & Llantrisant Corps - 3 Troops - Major R.F.Rickards
Cardiff Troop - 1 Troop- Captain Whitlock Nicholl

From 22-30 December 1824, the Central and Llantrisant Troops provided detachments for duty on Sker beach to protect the hull, fittings and cargo of a wreck from the activities of what one might term 'local opportunists'.

On the 14 May, 1825, a detachment of the Central and Llantrisant Cavalry consisting of:

Lt Joseph May of the Llantrisant Corps
Quartermaster Thomas Evans of Newcastle
Sergeant Major Timothy Castles of Bridgend
Sergeant Richard Lewis of Merthyr Mawr
Corporal Thomas Rees of Parcau
Corporal William Powell of Tythegston
Trumpeter David Major of Bridgend
Pte William Thomas of Bridgend
Pte William Hopkin of Bridgend

Headpiece and badge of a shako of the Eastern Glamorgan Yeomanry Cavalry, c1830. [Swansea Museum]

Pte Isaac Nicholas of Bridgend
Pte Llewelyn Jones of Bridgend
Pte Robert Williams of Bridgend
Pte Edmund Walters of Bridgend
Pte Thomas Williams of Llangerfedd
Pte Jno Lewis of Llangerfedd
Pte William Harry of Laleston
Pte David Lewis of Laleston

were called out in aid of the civil power at Bridgend. Fortunately no offensive action became necessary, their presence, once it became known, being sufficient to restore the King's Peace. Further West, the Swansea and Fairwood Troops commanded by Major Hughes assembled for permanent duty in Swansea on 6 June during which period their band created great interest amongst the townspeople. The *Cambrian,* reporting the event a day or so after their dismissal, said:

The Swansea and Fairwood Troops of Yeomanry completed their eight days of permanent duty on Tuesday last, and we have to remark that the orderly and steady conduct of the men during that period earned praise from the inhabitants as well as evinced the sedulous attention of their Officers to their discipline and improvement. Their respected Commander, Major Hughes, on dismissing the Troops, thanked them for their good behaviour while embodied, and recommended a similar course on their being dismissed. The Men gave him three hearty cheers in return and then separated. The fine state of the weather during the duty attracted many spectators to watch their evolutions. The improved state of discipline has been greatly facilitated by Captain Penrice of the 1st Troop. [11]

At Bridgend, the Central and Llantrisant Troops assembled for the like purpose on 31 July for eight days. Present were:

Major R F Rickards (Major Commandant)

Captain John Nicholl	1st Central Troop
Captain C R M Talbot	2nd Central Troop
Captain John Richards	Llantrisant Troop
Lt Charles Morgan	1st Central Troop
Lt Griffith Llewelyn	2nd Central Troop
Lt Joseph May	Llantrisant Troop
Cornet J Lloyd Vaughan Watkins	1st Central Troop
Cornet Robert Hillier Rickards	Llantrisant Troop

2 Quartermasters
1 Sergeant Major
8 Sergeants
8 Corporals
2 Trumpeters
158 Privates.

Although the name of Cornet Rickards is included in the Return for the July 1825 training, later correspondence shows that he was never at any time in attendance. The fact that his name was entered on the Return and Pay and Allowances drawn in his name for service not rendered, was later to become amongst other things the cause of great dispute and bring to an abrupt end the union between the Central Troops and Llantrisant Troop of Yeomanry Cavalry.

Such matters however were of little concern to the gentility of Bridgend, who enjoyed immensely the social activity brought on by the presence in town of the Yeomanry.

Bridgend last week presented an unusual scene of gaiety and attraction, and the Central Glamorgan Yeomanry under the command of Major Rickards acquitted themselves highly to the satisfaction of their Officers and the inhabitants of the town and the neighbourhood.

Lieutenant May of Cae Vatry opined that a finer set of men never appeared in the Field. [12]

However, a storm was brewing and gathered strength towards the end of the year. As early as October 1824, Captain John Nicholl of Merthyr Mawr had pointed out to Major Rickards certain inaccuracies in the Returns for Pay and Allowances which he was as Major Commandant submitting to the War Office for payment on behalf of the Central and Llantrisant Troops. Receiving no explanation from Major Rickards, and noting that no correction had been made to the documents concerned, John Nicholl continued to press the matter after the July 1825 training, adding that he was most unhappy to note that pay and allowances were being claimed for Cornet Rickards, when to the full knowledge of the Major (his Father), the young man was at the time many thousands of miles away in India.

The correspondence which was exchanged on the matter was considerable and became more tense and unpleasant as the months passed by. Refusing to be put off with weak explanations and excuses John Nicholl's kettle of discontent slowly came to the boil, but it was not until 1827 that the lid blew off and so came close to creating a county scandal.

In August 1826, the Swansea and Fairwood Troops provided an escort for the Duke of Gloucester on the occasion of his visit to Swansea. Having delivered the royal personage safely to Woodlands Castle, the Detachment were then inspected, on completion of which the officers in turn were presented. In September, the West Glamorgan Troops assembled in Swansea for eight days training, whilst at Bridgend a somewhat unhappy Central and Llantrisant Cavalry were drawn out for the same purpose. At Swansea, the local Yeomanry Cavalry Troops were inspected by Major Chatterton, 4th Dragoon Guards who expressed his appreciation of their soldierlike appearance and the regularity and precision of their field movements.[13] Further east in Cardiff, Whitlock Nicholl's Troop were also engaged in similar activity.

Meanwhile the dispute between Captain Nicholl of the 1st Central Troop and Major Rickards continued and became more heated, with the result that in March 1827 the Major tendered his resignation to the Lord Lieutenant. The reaction of the Marquis of Bute in the circumstances was rather surprising as, far from supporting Captain Nicholl's case, he, for reasons best known to himself, found no fault in the Major and considered that his resignation would be injurious to the good name of the county. At this stage, Major Rickards much heartened by the support given to him by the Marquis of Bute, received that gentleman's permission to resign as commandant of the Central and Llantrisant corps and to terminate the union which had brought the two groups together.

The Marquis after correspondence with the War Office received the following reply from Sir Robert Peel on 23 August, 1827:

I have laid before the King the former part of your Lordship's letter of the 15th instant tendering the resignation of Mr Rickards, Commandant of the Central Corps of

Yeomanry Cavalry, and requesting that the Llantrisant Corps be separated from that Corps, and I am to acquaint your Lordship that His Majesty is graciously pleased to approve thereof.

The knowledge that Rickards was to continue to serve in the County Yeomanry as Captain of the Llantrisant Troop with the Lord Lieutenant's support, was too bitter a pill for John Nicholl to accept and he tendered his resignation as senior Captain of the two Central Troops but, on a plea from the Lord Lieutenant, he agreed that it should not take effect until after the autumn training and the appointment of a suitable successor. True to his word, he continued to hold the reins of command until such matters were settled. In about January 1830 he was succeeded by Charles Morgan, Esq, of Ruperra, Monmouthshire.

Formation of the Eastern Corps, Glamorgan Yeomanry

In February 1828, the Llantrisant and Cardiff Troops of Yeomanry Cavalry were united to form the Eastern Glamorgan Yeomanry Cavalry under the command of Major Richard Fowler Rickards who, in spite of past questionable conduct, had emerged from the fray remarkably unscathed.

Acceptance of the new corps was confirmed by the Secretary of State for War in a letter to the Marquis of Bute dated 28 February 1828, which also set the establishment at: 1 major, 3 captains, 3 lieutenants, 3 cornets, 3 quartermasters, 1 sergeant major, 6 sergeants, 6 corporals, 3 trumpeters and 150 private men.

Amongst additional officers appointed and gazetted on 19 March were:

Lieutenant John Moggridge
Lt Mathew Moggridge
Cornet David Hopkin
Cornet Lewis Reece

On paper therefore, the strength of the Glamorgan Yeomanry Corps on 31 March, 1828, stood at :

Swansea and Fairwood	-	3 Troops
Central Glamorgan	-	2 Troops
Eastern Glamorgan	-	3 Troops

The Eastern Troops were dressed in similar fashion to the Central and Western corps but with certain minor differences. There is preserved in the Swansea Museum part of a shako worn by an officer of the Eastern corps. All that remains is the headpiece of black beaver cloth, around the crown of which is a 2" wide band of silver lace with silver lions heads and rings through which the cap lines were at one time threaded. The badge on the front is not an universal pattern, but one specifically designed for the East Glamorgan Troops. It consists of a garter belt inscribed 'Eastern Glamorgan Yeomanry' within which lie the plumes, coronet and motto scrolls, viz, the badge of the Prince of Wales - the whole embroidered in gold and silver wire and other coloured threads. The headpiece appears to fit the design of what is described in W Y Carman's book on cavalry head-dress [14] as the Light Dragoon 1830 pattern, and therefore unlike the shako worn by the officers of the Central corps, conforms to the new Dress Regulations prompted by William IV in 1830 which confined gold ornaments and lace to the dress of officers of the regular army.

In 1829, the Swansea and Fairwood Troops came out for 8 days permanent duty in Swansea commencing on 8 June under the command of Major Thomas Penrice who had succeeded the long serving and respected Major Edward Hughes. At Bridgend, the Central Troops were similarly occupied as were the Eastern Troops in Cardiff. All three groups were inspected when training by Colonel Jackson of the 6th Dragoon Guards and with good results. Having inspected the Eastern Troops on the 16 June, the Colonel

... was pleased to express himself in high terms of commendation at the extraordinary precision with which the manoeuvres were performed and of the soldierlike appearance of the Corps generally. [15]

The conduct of the three divisions whilst in quarters was as usual exemplary. At Swansea on 2 July, the Western Troops took part in the proclamation parade on the accession of William IV. The procession was led by the sergeant major and 6 file dismounted. Behind, a trumpeter flanked by two farriers carrying axes. Then came the band of the Swansea Cavalry followed by the magistrates, the corporation, the leading inhabitants of the town and a detachment of cavalry. The procession was flanked by dismounted members of the corps.

On 11 August, the Western Troops commanded by Major Penrice completed 8 days permanent duty in Swansea, whilst at Cowbridge the Central Troops were similarly engaged. All three divisions were inspected during the course of the month by Major Wyndham of the Scots Greys with good results.

The Central Glamorgan Yeomanry commanded by Captain Morgan were reviewed on Monday night at Cowbridge by Major Wyndham of the Scots Greys. The Corps went through the evolutions in a soldierlike manner, Captain Talbot, our County Member was in the Field at the head of his Troop. A finer set of young men we have not seen for some time. The major part of them are the sons of respectable Farmers. [16]

The Merthyr Insurrection of June 1831

In June 1831 there occurred in Merthyr Tydfil a civil disturbance of such ferocity, the like of which had never previously been experienced in Wales. Sparked off at Aberdare on 1 June, the rioting spread the next day to Merthyr Tydfil where iron production was brought to a standstill and such forces of law and order as existed found themselves helpless and unable to calm the fury of the mob.

In response to an appeal to the Lord Lieutenant for assistance, military forces, both regular and auxiliary, were alerted. First to respond was the Officer Commanding troops at Brecon and, by 10 the next morning (Friday, 3 June) a detachment of the 93rd (Sutherland) Highlanders arrived at the Cyfarthfa Iron Works.

In Cardiff, the Militia staff and a detachment of the Royal Glamorgan Light Infantry Militia were withdrawn from annual training and bundled into coaches post haste for Merthyr. In Cardiff, Bridgend and Swansea, the three divisions of the Glamorgan Yeomanry corps were embodied with orders to proceed with all speed and by the shortest route to the scene.

Meanwhile in Merthyr, a pitched battle had taken place between the 93rd Highlanders and the rioters outside the Castle Inn. An attempt by some of the boldest protesters to disarm the soldiers ended disastrously.

Ordered to open fire on the mob, the soldiers complied, and many of the crowd were killed or seriously wounded. Several soldiers were also injured, two of them seriously, whilst others were disarmed. Later in the day, the arrival in the town of 50 officers and men of the Glamorgan Militia, together with Major Rickards' Eastern Division of the Glamorgan Yeomanry allowed a short breathing space. With those reinforcements to hand, the military withdrew from the town centre to set up headquarters and a defensive perimeter at Penydarren House and no further confrontation took place that day.

On Saturday 4 June, Captain Moggridge of the Eastern Division Glamorgan Yeomanry set off with a detachment of 40 men to meet and escort the baggage and ammunition waggons of the 93rd that were then approaching the town from Brecon. As the yeomanry column passed through the deep ravine at Cefn Coed y Cymmer, Moggridge found himself hemmed in by rioters whilst others perched on the high ground overlooking the ravine subjected the yeomen to a barrage of boulders and stones. When news of the ambush reached Lt Colonel Thomas Morgan, commanding the Glamorgan Yeomanry, who had just arrived at Penydarren with the Central Division, he at once ordered Major Rickards with 100 yeomen to the rescue. So strong were the rioters, and so intense the barrage of stones and sporadic musketry fire, that a break through proved impossible. Unable to deploy his men for a charge due to the restricted and rocky nature of the ground, Rickards had no alternative but to withdraw, but fortunately Moggridge had in the meantime extricated his troop at the expense of one man wounded and one disarmed. Undeterred, he moved on to meet the waggons and brought them safely into Merthyr the next day by a more circuitous but lesser known route.

By far the most serious set back suffered by the yeomanry that day took place on the road between Hirwaen and Merthyr which follows roughly the line of the present day Heads of the Valleys road between the two towns. There, Major Penrice, who was leading an advance guard of the Swansea and Fairwood Division towards Merthyr was, with a half-troop of 36 men, ambushed at a spot some two miles west of the town. The rioters, numbering several hundred and armed with a mixture of firearms and edged weapons, were aware of Penrice's approach and lay in wait in an area bordering the road littered with tips and mounds which gave them plenty of cover. As the yeomen drew near, Penrice, who had neglected to throw out scouts, was approached in the most friendly manner by one or two men and, whilst thus diverted, suddenly found himself and his half troop surrounded by a crowd who appeared out of cover. Pressing in close, they disarmed the yeomen and with that accomplished allowed them to retire via Hirwaen in the direction of Swansea. Nursing a badly wounded pride, Penrice and his men met up with the main body of the Western Division on the return journey and, having rearmed themselves chose wisely to approach Merthyr via Bridgend and Llantrisant, which reorganisation and journey did not allow them to arrive in Merthyr until early the next Monday morning.

In Merthyr, meanwhile the mob had advanced upon Penydarren, but finding the military prepared to give them a hot reception, had second thoughts and dispersed without any need of persuasion.

Sunday 5 June passed by quietly, but at 10am on the Monday, the mob once again moved in against the military. Being aware of this move, Lt Colonel Morgan (who by that time had at his disposal 110 officers and men of the 93rd, 50 officers and men of the Royal Glamorgan Militia and 300 yeomen from the Glamorgan Corps of Yeomanry) moved his force out to meet them. Accompanied by magistrates, the troops came face to face with the rioters at Dowlais Great Pond. After the ironmasters had appealed, in both English and Welsh, for the rioters to peacefully disperse, the Riot Act was read, but proved equally ineffective. Having exhausted all peaceful means the magistrates had no alternative but to place matters in the hands of the military. The Highlanders and the militia were ordered to load and the yeomanry (on this occasion well deployed and with room to manoeuvre) to draw their sabres. Words of command were given clearly to create maximum effect. The sound of 300 sabres clearing steel scabbards and the sight of some 150 muskets being brought to the ready, left no doubt as to the final intention. At the point when a second bloodbath seemed inevitable, the front rank of rioters gave way, others quickly followed and soon the exodus became general, assisted by the yeomanry who, pressing forward slowly, 'encouraged' stragglers to move faster with the flats of their sabres. The general feeling amongst the military was one of relief and satisfaction, particulary due to the fact that the operation had been accomplished without bloodshed. The Merthyr Insurrection was almost over, and ended later in the day when, following the arrival of regular cavalry, the ringleaders were arrested and removed to

Cardiff under escort. On Wednesday 8 June, the Yeomanry rode out of Merthyr, the Swansea and Fairwood Troops proceeding in some haste as news of disturbances in the Swansea district had been conveyed to them in a message from the Lord Lieutenant. Strike action and unrest amongst colliers in the Clydach and Cwm Tawe valleys kept them embodied until the 10 June when they were dismissed, a grateful Swansea Corporation voting them a shilling each with which to drink the King's health.

As was to be expected, the disarming of Major Penrice's half troop on the 4 June was to have repercussions. Within hours of the incident, the first of a mass of correspondence on the event was being written and exchanged. The opponents of yeomanry cavalry in the government, ably assisted by the press, magnified the incident out of all proportion by portraying the disarming of a half troop as a prime example of the unreliability of yeomanry cavalry. The critics chose to overlook not only the size and scale of the rioting which had taken place at Merthyr, the like of which had never been experienced elsewhere in Great Britain, but also the reliable service of some 250 other yeomen, whose sterling service received not a word of thanks or recognition. Major Penrice was required to produce a full report of the incident for the Lord Lieutenant and the Secretary of State, and later, accompanied by Captain Collins, attended at Merthyr to attempt to identify some of those involved in their disarming. On the 24th, the following letter from a Merthyr magistrate was published in the *Cambrian:*

> The Officers of the Swansea Cavalry attended at the Police Office, Merthyr on the 18th inst to identify several persons who are in custody on suspicion of disarming part of a Troop between Merthyr and Hirwaen on the 4th inst.
>
> A very full examination of the parties on both sides necessarily elicited clear proof that the whole of the armed insurgents had crossed the valley from Dan y Graig and were posted on the cinder tips ready for hostilities. The manner in which the Officers in advance were surprised under a mask of friendship and the men gradually hemmed in by a dense mass totally inextricable by Horses worn out with the labour of the day before, taken up from grass and thoroughly knocked up by a forced march from the Gower was satisfactorily proved.
>
> It gives me the greatest pleasure to record my opinion, that had a Troop of Regular Dragoons been so circumstanced (without the power of making a charge) they could not have acted otherwise.

An enquiry into the incident was requested, the proceedings commencing at Merthyr on the 25 July and continuing at Pyle five days later. Although accepting that Major Penrice had failed to take sufficient precautions by failing to throw out scouts, they concluded the investigation as follows:

> They do not consider that the slightest imputation or want of courage can be laid to the charge of either Officers or Men on this unfortunate occasion; but that on the contrary, they all evinced every disposition to do their duty to the utmost of their ability.

During July 1831 the Marquis of Bute in a report to the Secretary of State proposed that the yeomanry cavalry corps of Glamorgan be reorganised as a unit consisting of three troops, one each to be furnished by the Western, Central and Eastern Districts respectively, but that prior to the change the existing troops should be totally disbanded. His proposal was approved and the order for disbandment circulated to the officers commanding on the 22 August 1831. Accompanying the disbandment order was a letter which outlined government proposals for the reorganised corps.

On receipt of the disbandment order, commanding officers carried out the instructions, and the yeomanry corps of Glamorgan stood down on or about the 5 September 1831.

By disbanding prior to a reorganisation, as opposed to reducing the size of the existing corps, both government and Lord Lieutenant ensured the failure of the scheme. Reorganisation as proposed by the Marquis, was still under discussion in 1832, but those best fitted to organise and command the unit showed no interest, having formed the opinion that the changes were ill timed and that the disbandments reflected unfavourably on their personal reputations. Thus ended the first chapter of Glamorgan's yeomanry history. Their like were not to be seen again in the county for close on 70 years.

Officers of the Yeomanry Cavalry - September 1820

Swansea and Fairwood Troop

Major Edward Hughes	4 April 1814
Capt Robert Nelson Thomas	26 July 1804
Capt Hugh Powell Watkins	4 April 1814
Capt Herbert Edward Evans	1 June 1820
Lt John Griffiths Hancorne	9 January 1817
Lt Stephen Bowen Jones	14 December 1818
Lt Charles Collins	1 June 1820
Cornet John Davies	15 November 1818
Adjutant George Harries	24 December 1816
Surgeon John Davies	10 January 1817
Surgeon Charles Sylvester	10 January 1917

Cardiff Troop

Capt Whitlock Nicholl	21 May 1819

Central Glamorgan Troop

Capt John Nicholl	19 August 1820

As at September 20th, 1825

Swansea and Fairwood Troops

Major Edward Hughes	4 April 1814
Capt Herbert Edward Evans	1 June 1820
Captain Thomas Penrice	11 March 1822
Capt Charles Collins	31 May 1825
Lt John Griffiths Hancorne	9 January 1817
Lt Stephen Bowen Jones	14 December 1818
Lt Thomas Thomas	31 May 1825
Cornet John J Strick	31 May 1825
Adjutant George Harries	24 December 1816
Surgeon William Terry	1825

Cardiff Troop

Capt Whitlock Nicholl	21 May 1819
Lt Richard Wyndham Williams	16 May 1821
Cornet Henry Villiers Stuart	20 November 1824

Central Glamorgan Troops

Major Richard Fowler Rickards	22 October 1824
Capt John Nicholl	23 October 1824
Capt Christopher Rice Mansel Talbot	25 October 1824
Capt John Richards	29 June 1825
Lt Joseph May	26 October 1824
Lt Charles Morgan(Ruperra)	27 October 1824
Lt Griffith Llewelyn (Baglan)	28 October 1824
Cornet J Lloyd Vaughan Watkins	29 October 1824
Cornet Robert Hillier Rickards	22 November 1824

East Glamorgan Troops (Cardiff & Llantrisant)
(all appointed 19 February,1828)
Major Richard Fowler Rickards
Lt John Moggridge
Lt Mathew Moggridge
Cornet David Hopkin
Cornet Richard Lewis Rees.

Other Ranks - Yeomanry Nominal Lists

Swansea Troop - August 1819 (Bute MSS)

Sgt Wm Attwood	Swansea
Sgt Chapman	Swansea
Sgt Thos Davies	Swansea
Sgt Thos T Evans	Oystermouth
Sgt Joseph Gwynne	Swansea Parish
Sgt David Harry	Lougher
Cpl John Clarke Jnr	Llanddewi
Cpl Geo Gordon	Llanrhidian

Cpl Wm Hughes	Swansea Parish
Cpl Wm Rowlands	Ilston
Cpl Wm Watts	Swansea
Trumpeter Thos Griffiths	Swansea
Trumpeter Lionel Mawbey	Swansea
Farrier Edw Howell	Knelston
Pte Geo Ace	Reynoldston
Pte Geo Bennett	Oystermouth
Pte Geo Bevan	Penrice
Pte John Bowen	Cheriton
Pte John Button	Oystermouth
Pte Chas Clarke	Llanddewi
Pte John Clement	Llanddewi
Pte Wm Clement	Swansea
Pte David Daniels	Oystermouth
Pte John Daniels	Oystermouth
Pte Rees David	Llansamlet
Pte John Davies	Swansea
Pte Thos Davies	Neath
Pte Wm Davies	Llandeilo Talybont
Pte David Edwards	Lanedy
Pte Wm Edwards	Lanedy
Pte Benjamin Evans	Llansamlet
Pte Edw Evans	Swansea
Pte John Evans	Swansea
Pte John Evans	Cheriton
Pte Thos Evans	Swansea
Pte Thos Evans	Swansea Parish
Pte Wm Evans	Llansamlet
Pte Rowland Givelin	Pennard
Pte Richd Gregory	Llandeilo Talybont
Pte Joseph Griffith	Swansea
Pte Morgan Griffith	Lanedy
Pte John Guy	Cheriton
Pte John Harry	Swansea
Pte Thos Harry	Llangennech
Pte David Hopkin	Lanedy
Pte Richd Hopkin	Llandeilo Talybont
Pte Wm Hopkins	Llanelli
Pte Edw Hughes	Swansea
Pte Jenkin Jenkins	Swansea Parish
Pte John Jenkins	Oxwich
Pte Wm Jenkins	Oystermouth
Pte Evan John	Llandeilo Talybont
Pte Daniel Jones	Llanon
Pte Geo Jones	Llanrhidian

110

Pte John Jones	Swansea
Pte Joseph Jones	Swansea
Pte Morgan Jones	Llansamlet
Pte Morgan Jones	Llanon
Pte Wm Jones	Knelston
Pte Chris Lewis	Rhosilli
Pte John Lewis	Swansea
Pte Simon Lewis	Swansea
Pte John Long	Llanddewi
Pte Edw Mainwaring	Lanedy
Pte Wm Matthews	Llandeilo Talybont
Pte Daniel Morgan	Lanedy
Pte David Morgan	Swansea
Pte Rees Morgan	Llansamlet
Pte Thos Morris	Swansea Parish
Pte Thos Nicholls	Oystermouth
Pte Griffith Owen	Oystermouth
Pte Morgan Owen	Llanon
Pte David Owens	Lanedy
Pte Daniel Phillips	Llanddewi
Pte Rich Phillips	Oystermouth
Pte John Rees	Llanelli
Pte Morgan Rees	Swansea
Pte Morgan Rice	Knelston
Pte Wm Roper	Swansea Parish
Pte John Rothero	Llanddewi
Pte Geo Thomas	Llanrhidian
Pte Thos Thomas	Llansamlet
Pte Wm Thomas	Lanedy
Pte Thos Thomlinson	Swansea
Pte Phillip Walters	Reynoldston
Pte John Wilks	Llansamlet
Pte David Williams	Swansea
Pte John Williams	Swansea Parish
Pte John Williams	Oystermouth
Pte Wm Williams	Llandeilo Talybont
Pte Joseph Wood	Swansea

Fairwood Troop - August 1819 (Bute MSS)

Sgt Thos Evans	Swansea
Sgt Henry Jones	Swansea
Sgt Wm Wilkins	Llanrhidian
Cpl John John	Llanelli
Cpl David Smith	Cilybebyll
Trumpeter Thos Bishop	Swansea
Farrier Wm Richards	Swansea

Pte Geo Beynon	Swansea
Pte Geo Beynon	Llangenith
Pte Thos Bowen	Swansea
Pte Thos Bowen	Llanrhidian
Pte Rich Clarke	Llangenith
Pte John Clement	Llandeilo Talybont
Pte Roger David	Cilybebyll
Pte Wm David	Llanrhidian
Pte John Davies	Llanrhidian
Pte David Eaton	Llanelli
Pte Wm Evan	Swansea Parish
Pte Francis Francis	Bishopston
Pte Henry Griffith	Llandeilo Talybont
Pte Henry Griffith	Swansea
Pte David Gwelin	Ilston
Pte Saml Havard	Swansea
Pte Wm Harries	Swansea
Pte David Hopkin	Swansea
Pte Wm Hopkin	Llandeilo Talybont
Pte John Howell	Swansea
Pte Thos Hughes	Swansea Parish
Pte David James	Llanelli
Pte David Jenkins	Swansea
Pte Wm John	Swansea
Pte John Jones	Bettws
Pte Joseph Jones	Swansea
Pte Morgan Jones (1)	Llangyfelach
Pte Morgan Jones (2)	Llangyfelach
Pte Thos Jones	Swansea
Pte John Lewis	Swansea
Pte Francis Morgan	Swansea
Pte Rich Morgan	Swansea
Pte Wm Morgan	Llanrhidian
Pte John Morris	Swansea
Pte Wm Morris	Bettws
Pte Wm Morris	Llanelli
Pte John Parry	Bishopston
Pte Thos Perkins	Swansea Parish
Pte John Rees	Llandeilo Talybont
Pte Morgan Rees	Bettws
Pte Sinclair Rees	Reynoldston
Pte David Rogers	Llangyfelach
Pte Jas Roper	Swansea Parish
Pte Wm Taylor	Rhosilli
Pte David Thomas	Llanrhidian
Pte John Thomas	Swansea

Pte Thos Thomas	Pennard
Pte Thos Thomas	Bishopston
Pte Thos Thomas	Llangyfelach
Pte Wm Thomas	Llanelli
Pte Rich Townshend	Neath
Pte John Wiggins	Swansea
Pte Henry Williams	Llanelli
Pte Joseph Williams	Reynoldston
Pte Thos Williams	Llandeilo Talybont

It is of interest to note that the recruiting catchment district for both troops extended from Neath to the East, through Swansea Town and the Gower, to Llanelli in Carmarthenshire.

Central Glamorgan Cavalry
Return of Captain Nicholl's and Captain Talbot's Troops - August 3 1827

Captain Nicholl	
QM Thos Evans	Newcastle
Sgt Thos Hiscock	Cowbridge
Sgt John Jones	Ogmore
Sgt Rich Lewis	Merthyr Mawr
Sgt John Sands	Llandough
Cpl John John	Brynmenyn
Cpl Thos Stanford	Wick
Pte Evan Bevan	Tribyn
Pte John Butler	Shelf
Pte Thos Butler	Coychurch
Pte Saml David	Brynglas
Pte Thos David	Oldcastle
Pte David Davies	Coity
Pte Rees Hawkins	Tymaes
Pte Thos Hopkin	Llwyn y Brain
Pte Wm Hopkin	Gellilaes
Pte Rich Howell	Candleston
Pte Thos Howell	Giblat
Pte David James	Bettws
Pte Edw James	Tondu
Pte David Jenkins	Newcastle
Pte John Jones	St Brides
Pte Llewelyn Jones	Bridgend
Pte Thos Llewelyn	Bridgend
Pte David Major	Bridgend
Pte Evan Martin	Newcastle
Pte Thos Mathews	Watertown Ct
Pte Thos Morgan	Pitcot
Pte Saml Morgan	Newcastle

Pte Evan Nicholas	Pencoed
Pte Isaac Nicholas	Bridgend
Pte David Rees	Ty'n y Pant
Pte Thos Roberts	Coity
Pte Anthony Stew	Cae
Pte David Thomas	Pant yr Awel
Pte John Thomas (1)	Wick
Pte John Thomas (2)	Wick
Pte Rich Thomas	Garwa
Pte Thos Thomas	Broadway
Pte Wm Thomas	Bridgend
Pte Wm Thomas	Merthyr Mawr
Pte Edmund Walters	Bridgend
Pte Phillip Walters	Coity
Pte Robt Williams	Oldcastle
Pte Wm Yorath	Coity
Captain Talbot	
QM Edw Burnell	Newton
Sgt Evan Morgan	Cornelly
Sgt Wm Powell	Eglwysnewydd
Sgt Thos Rees	Parcae
Sgt John Williams	Sker
Cpl Watkin Bevan	Newton
Cpl John Joseph	Croeswen
Cpl David Lewis	Laleston
Cpl Wm Powell	Tythegston
Cpl Rich Roberts	Newmill Bridge
Pte Craddock Burnell	Nottage
Pte Thos Burnell	Newton
Pte Rees David	Newcastle
Pte Wm David	Newton
Pte Thos Edwards	Dyffryn
Pte Robt Evans	Newton
Pte Wm Harry	Laleston
Pte Thos Henry	Newton
Pte Thos Hopkin	Nottage
Pte David Howell	Cornelly
Pte David Howell	Stormy
Pte John Howell	Penmynydd
Pte Rich Howell	Grove
Pte Wm Howell	Newton
Pte Thos Jenkins	Ty Talwyn
Pte David Jones	Newton
Pte Geo Jones	Ballas
Pte John Lewis	Llangenydd

Pte Wm Lewis	Laleston
Pte John Morgan	Somerset House
Pte R John Morgan	Stormy
Pte Edw Powell	Slade
Pte John Rhoderick	Newlands
Pte John Richards	Lower Court
Pte Edmund Sanders	Cornelly
Pte David Thomas	Newton
Pte Isaac Thomas	Danygraig
Pte Jenkin Thomas	Nottage
Pte Rees Thomas	Newton
Pte Rees Thomas	Kenfig
Pte Thos Thomas	Cwm
Pte Wm Thomas	Craigoch
Pte Wm Thomas	Cefncribwr
Pte Thos Williams	Llangenydd
Pte Thos Williams	Newton (later Tythegston)

Other Rolls and Returns can be found in the Merthyr Mawr MSS and in my book *Glamorgan its Gentlemen & Yeomanry.*

NOTES

1. *Cambrian* ,10 June 1808.
2. *Cambrian,* 2 December 1808.
3. *Cambrian,* 16 June 1809.
4. *Cambrian* ,8 June 1810.
5. Later 2nd Bn, The Border Regt.
6. *Cambrian,* 20 November 1818.
7. *Cambrian,* 26 November 1819
8. *Cambrian,* 11 February 1820.
9. *Cambrian,* 28 July 1820.
10. Bute Papers.
11. *Cambrian,* 17 June 1825.
12. *Cambrian,* 12 August 1825.
13. *Cambrian,* 22 September 1826.
14. Carman,W Y, *Head-Dress of the British Army - Cavalry,* Woolwich 1968.
15. *Cambrian* ,19 June 1829.
16. *Cambrian,* 20 August 1830.

Appendix 1
Archival Sources and Avenues for Further Research

National Library of Wales
    Penrice & Margam MSS – Reference to Glamorgan Provisional Cavalry.

National Museum of Wales (Welsh Folk Museum)
    Farming and Rural Life Collection – Perkins Diary, reference to Glamorgan
    Provisional Cavalry.

Public Record Office
    ADM/ 28 Sea Fencibles
    Pay Lists 1798-1810.

    WO1/942 & HO 513151, Provisional Cavalry, Formation, Disbandment etc
    of the corps, 1797-1800.

    WO 2/1 Lists of Volunteer Corps and index to correspondence concerning same,
    1794-1796.

    WO 4/158 (105-106) Volunteer formations, 1793-95.

    WO 6/197-202 Formation of Volunteer Corps. Continuation of services of and
    related instructions, 1798-1803.

    WO 6/199 Volunteer Corps - formation, conditions of service, pay and
    allowances, related correspondence, 1798-99.

    WO 13 Volunteer Records (including Pay and Muster lists).

    WO 34/155 Offers of Cities and Boroughs to raise Volunteer Corps in
    National Emergency, 1799.

    WO 40/10 Returns of various Volunteer Regiments, 1795-98.

    HO 50/458 Lists of Volunteer Corps 1797.

    HO 51/151-157 Formations, Establishments, Volunteer Corps, 1796-1806.

National Library of Wales, English XVIII-XIX.9665E
    List of persons who supplied horses to the Swansea Yeomanry Cavalry,
    1799-1803.

    Return of Swansea, Gowerland & Kilvey Legion, 25 September - 6 December
    1800.

    Notice 3 May 1803. Lt Colonel Thomas Morgan to the Swansea Cavalry.

Invoice 10 September 1803, from Edward Davies, London, for military
equipment.

Glamorgan County Records Office (Cardiff)
Company Order Book, Captain Evans' Company, Swansea Fuzileers.

The Bute Papers.

Lieutenancy documents relating to the Glamorgan Cavalry and Infantry
Volunteers.

Merthyr Mawr Papers.

Newspapers
The Cambrian
The Hereford Journal
The Gloucester Journal

Published Works

Fortesque, J W,   Barstow, 'Sea Fencibles', *Guns, Weapons & Militaria, Vol 1*, No 11,
October 1982.

Cousins, G,   *The Defenders*, London, 1968.

Fortesque, J W,   *The History of the British Army, Vol IV*, London, 1921.
Journal of the Society for Army Historical Research, Vol XXXI,
'Provisional Cavalry, 1797-1800', No 128, Winter 1953.

The County Lieutenancies and the Army, 1803-1814, London, 1909.
'The Volunteer Army of Great Britain, 1806', Marquis of Cambridge,
Journal of the Society for Army Historical Research, Vol XXXI,
Nos 127 & 128.

Haythorn-
thwaite, P J,   'The Volunteer Force 1803-04' *Journal of the Society for
Army Historical Research, Vol LXIV*, No 260.

Jones, D   *Before Rebecca*, London, 1973.

Penrice, Thomas, *Copy of the Order Book of the Swansea & Fairwood Yeomanry
Cavalry*, 1831.

Wilkins, C   *The History of Merthyr Tydfil*, Merthyr Tydfil, 1867.

Williams, G A,   *The Merthyr Rising*, London, 1978.

List of Officers of the Local Militia of Great Britain, War Office, 1810.

*Yeomanry & Volunteer Cavalry Lists, 1794-97; 1799-1801; 1803-05;
1807; 1817; 1820; 1825.*

Parliamentary Session Papers.

Yeomanry & Volunteer Cavalry Returns. (these contain a mass of information which covers the period 1797-1850, and in particular the year 1803. Included are Establishments, effective Strengths, Expenses, Call Outs in Aid of Civil Power, Reduction in Strength, etc).

Index

Personal names which appear in the text are included in this index but those which appear in nominal roles for various units are not recorded here. Figures in italics denote an illustration.

122

124

Other military titles by Bridge Books

VCs of Wales and the Welsh Regiments
W Alister Williams

Biographical details of 81 recipients of the Victoria Cross who were from Wales or who served with regiments now associated with the Principality. Fully illustrated with 167 photographs (many never previously published). Appearing in 1984, this book is now regarded as the standard reference work on the subject. ISBN 0-9508285-4-8.   Casebound.

North Wales in the Civil War
Norman Tucker

Privately published in the 1950s, this book contains a wealth of detail and remains unsurpassed as a highly readable description of the Civil War in North Wales. Although no major battles took place in the region there were a number of seiges and large scale skirmishes which are all detailed in this volume. ISBN 1-872424-24-4   Softback.

Victim of Circumstance
Michael Paziuk

Subtitled *A Ukranian in the Army of the Third Reich*, this book tells the story of a 16 year old boy's experiences after being pressed into service in the enemy's army, to serve a regime that was totally alien to him. He served on two fronts and was wounded before being taken prisoner of war and interned in Italy to await his fate as decreed by the Allied powers. ISBN 1-872424-32-5   Softback.

Available soon
Albert Ball, VC – Chaz Bowyer
Wings Over the Somme, 1916-1918 – Gwilym H Lewis, DFC
Further volumes in the series *History of the Welsh Militia and Volunteer Corps, 1757-1908*

Write for a catalogue to: Bridge Books, 61 Park Avenue, Wrexham, Clwyd, LL12 7AW